HOME IS THE HUNTER

Helen MacINNES

HOME IS
THE HUNTER

TITAN BOOKS

Home is the Hunter
Print edition ISBN: 9781781163313
E-book edition ISBN: 9781781164334

Published by Titan Books
A division of Titan Publishing Group Ltd
144 Southwark Street, London SE1 0UP

First edition: February 2014
1 2 3 4 5 6 7 8 9 10

A CIP catalogue record for this title is available from the British Library.

Printed and bound in Great Britain by CPI Group Ltd.

What did you think of this book?
We love to hear from our readers. Please email us at:
readerfeedback@titanemail.com, or write to us at the above address.

To receive advance information, news, competitions, and exclusive offers
online, please sign up for the Titan newsletter on our website.

www.titanbooks.com

**To the Angel
who will appear, some day**

CHARACTERS
(in order of appearance)

ATHENA
Goddess of Reason

ULYSSES
A hero of the Trojan War

EUMAEUS (Yu-MAY-us)
The swineherd

CLIA (CLEE-A)
Ulysses' old nurse, now maid to Penelope

AMARYLLIS (AMA-RILL-IS)
One of the three maidservants in the House of Ulysses

PENELOPE
Wife of Ulysses

TELEMACHUS (TEL-EM-ACUS)
Son of Ulysses

MELAS (MEE-LAS)
One of Penelope's suitors

ERYX
Another of the suitors

HOMER
Poet

PHILETIUS (FIL-EET-IUS)
The stableman

SOME OTHER SUITORS

THE PLACE IS ITHACA, GREECE.
THE TIME IS 1177 B.C.
THE ACTION OCCURS IN, OR NEAR, THE HOUSE OF ULYSSES,
ON THE DAY OF HIS RETURN HOME.

ACT I

SCENE 1
On the road to Ulysses' House. Dawn

SCENE 2
Penelope's room. Early morning

SCENE 3
Penelope's room. Later that morning

ACT II

SCENE 1
The Great Hall of Ulysses' House. Early afternoon

SCENE 2
The same. Later that afternoon

SCENE 3
The same. That evening

ACT I

SCENE 1

By the dim light of dawn, just beginning, we can see a small shack huddled at one side of the stage, but everything else is shadowed and dark. Across the stage, a spot of light strengthens, and ATHENA, *Goddess of Reason, limps delicately into view. She wears a long white pleated robe as a Goddess should, but the long scarf attached to one shoulder is trailing, and the circlet of golden leaves on her high-piled hair is a little askew. She looks exhausted.*

ATHENA
(Sighing, as she looks back over her shoulder)

Oh, come on, Ulysses! You've rushed all the way from the harbour, not a thought in your head, nothing but silly emotions. "I'm home, I'm home!" you kept saying. Then, "What's wrong, what's wrong?" you kept asking.

(Her voice changes from joy to worry, as she mimics ULYSSES, *who enters and halts, looking across at the shack.*

*He is a tall man, handsome, in his late thirties. A long
rough cape is pushed back from his shoulders, to show a
simple tunic, a plain leather belt, an inconspicuous knife
at his waist. He carries a battered hat in one hand.)*

Well, you're right on both counts, my friend. You *are* home.
And there *is* something wrong.

*(ULYSSES walks past ATHENA, quite unaware of her, for
she is invisible to mortal men. The closest they come to
seeing Reason is to listen to her, but her words seem only
a part of their interior monologues, of the battle in their
minds. ULYSSES halts again, eying the shack, frowning.)*

Go on, Ulysses! Find out what *is* the trouble. But don't blame
me—I had nothing to do with it. I can't deal with the irrational.
I am only the Goddess of Reason!

*(She looks down at her dress, then speaks to the
audience with wry amusement, as she drapes the scarf
back into place.)*

Yes, I am Athena. But who would believe it after that mad rush
from the harbour?

(She straightens the circlet of leaves.)

He wouldn't listen to one word I said.—Or did he?

*(For ULYSSES has pulled the cape around him, settled the
hat over his eyes, stooped a little as he approaches the
door of the shack.)*

He did, he *did* listen!

*(She smiles delightedly, steps slowly back into the
darkness, merges with the deep shadows.)*

ULYSSES
(Softly)

Anyone at home?

> *(Silence. He takes a step toward the doorway.)*

EUMAEUS

(The swineherd, who calls this shack his home, springs from the dark doorway with a knife in his hands. He is old, ugly, wiry, and dangerous. He circles slowly around ULYSSES.*)*

No, you don't! Thought you'd sneak up on an old man and finish him off in the dark?

ULYSSES

(Standing very still, raising his empty hands)

I was only looking for a place to rest... Why should I kill you? You haven't much to steal—

EUMAEUS

That's for sure. So why are you here?

ULYSSES

I heard you kept the pigs and chickens for the big house up on the hill. Ulysses' house.

EUMAEUS

There isn't a pig left, and only a couple of chickens. You aren't getting them! So clear out! That's the road to the harbour! Do your begging in the village.

ULYSSES

I didn't come to beg.

EUMAEUS

So—they *did* send you to kill me. The way they killed Penelope's servants, one by one, secretly, in the dark, and threw their bodies off the cliff. Then they told everyone the men had deserted, run off, taken a ship for the mainland and—

ULYSSES

They? Who are *they*?

EUMAEUS

A bit of an actor, are you? Go on, start moving out.
(*He gestures angrily with his knife.*)

ULYSSES

But I've just arrived, here, in Ithaca. Got off the boat this morning, an hour ago. I'm a stranger looking for—

EUMAEUS

You won't find it here. What brought you sneaking along the shore to *my* door, anyway?

ULYSSES

I was on my way to the Big House. I thought I'd get food and shelter, there. Ulysses always made any stranger welcome.

EUMAEUS
(*Less suspicious, now*)

Ulysses isn't there. Hasn't been for years. Never did get back from the Trojan War.

ULYSSES

But his wife, Penelope—doesn't she still live there? She would give a stranger a place to sleep, some bread, and wine—

EUMAEUS

You'll get more than that.

ULYSSES

Such as what?

EUMAEUS

Insults and blows—if you keep your mouth shut. Death—if you try to help the lady Penelope.

ULYSSES

What?

EUMAEUS

Didn't anyone tell you, back in the village?

ULYSSES

They all seemed frightened. Wouldn't say much... That's why I came here. Thought I had better find out what's wrong, before I went to Ulysses' house.

EUMAEUS

What's wrong?
  (He crows with bitter laughter, sheathes his knife at his waist.)
Wrong... I could talk with you from now until sunset, and still wouldn't have told you the half of it. Don't go near that house.

Get back to the harbour, take the first ship out. Get away from this island.

ULYSSES

Why don't you take your own advice? You could slip away, now. There's a ship leaving this noon.

EUMAEUS

I've thought of it, don't think I haven't. I've thought of it for these last three years—since they came here, and took over, and—

ULYSSES
(Grimly serious)

They? Who *are* they?

EUMAEUS

It's no business of yours. Get out, while you're still alive. That's good advice. It's all I can give you.

ULYSSES
(Pretending to leave)

Why don't you come with me, old man? There isn't much to keep you here.

EUMAEUS

I'm not running out. Penelope—I'm not leaving her alone. I'm not leaving her son. I can't do much. But at least, I don't desert them.

ULYSSES

As Ulysses did?

EUMAEUS
(Angry)

Ulysses was my friend.

ULYSSES

Was?

EUMAEUS

He's dead.

ULYSSES

Are you sure?

EUMAEUS

Yes.

ULYSSES

What if he isn't?

EUMAEUS

Then he'd be here.

ULYSSES

Perhaps he is as big a coward as he was a fool. Perhaps he heard of *them*, whoever they are, and—

EUMAEUS
(Whipping out his knife again)

You're double my height and half my age, but you don't call Ulysses a coward.

ULYSSES

He was certainly a fool to stay away so long.

EUMAEUS

That wasn't his choosing! He would never forget Penelope.

ULYSSES

Forget her? No... Not that... He forgot time. So that makes him a very great fool—

EUMAEUS
(Threatening)

No man calls him that!

ULYSSES
(Catching EUMAEUS' *arm, knocking the knife to the ground)*

Not even Ulysses?
(He throws his cloak open, takes off his hat, stands erect. EUMAEUS *stares unbelievingly.)*

EUMAEUS

That grip is the same—but it can't be—it can't—

ULYSSES
(As EUMAEUS *still stares,* ULYSSES *points to the outside of his leg, where a scar runs above and below the knee.)*

Recognise this scar?
(He claps EUMAEUS *on the shoulder.)*

Yes, it's still the same old Ulysses. A bit older. That's all.

EUMAEUS

(Recovering)

Seventeen years older.

ULYSSES

(Amused, as EUMAEUS *suddenly grabs him and begins to laugh)*

As long as that? Yes, I suppose it is. Ten years at Troy, seven years wandering—Eumaeus, stop that—stop it! Hold on, there. You'll have everyone come running—quiet, now, quiet! Take it easy. I'm home—home to stay.

(He frees himself from the hysterical welcome. He grins, takes a seat on the ground, his back against the shack's wall.)

EUMAEUS

Yes, the same old Ulysses, playing his damned tricks.

(He squats down near ULYSSES, *and studies him.)*

But why play one on me? Didn't you trust me?

ULYSSES

I had to make sure of you. Everyone is changed. The minute I stepped off the ship, this morning, I knew something was wrong. I kept silent, told no one who I was, listened, and looked. I didn't like what I saw. It's a dead village.

EUMAEUS

It's a frightened village. They close their doors and shutter their windows, whenever they see a ship coming into the harbour.

ULYSSES

But why? They used to welcome strangers. This island used to be a friendly place.

EUMAEUS

No more, Ulysses. No more. When people are scared, they turn selfish, keep to themselves. We've had enough of strangers coming here, pretending to be honest travellers, pleasant young men—

ULYSSES

Young men?

EUMAEUS

—until they got their grip on the whole island, and took what they wanted.

ULYSSES

Took?

EUMAEUS

Everything and everyone—some by persuasion, some by promises, some by threats. Except Penelope. She has held out against them.

ULYSSES
(Worriedly)

She is well? She's safe?

EUMAEUS

Barely.

ULYSSES

What do you mean?

EUMAEUS

For three years, the men have been living in the Big House.

ULYSSES

Penelope let these men into my house? God damn it, what the hell was she doing?

EUMAEUS

Strangers were always welcomed into your house, Ulysses. That was your custom.

ULYSSES

But, a bunch of—

EUMAEUS

And who was to throw them out, when they stayed on—and on—and on? Your son was only fourteen when they arrived.

ULYSSES

My son... Did they kill him?

EUMAEUS

Some of them planned that, but it didn't come off. Thanks to Penelope. She has managed to keep him—and the rest of us—alive. He's a good lad, but useless against eleven men.

ULYSSES
(Slowly)

And how did Penelope manage all that?

EUMAEUS

She used her head, that's how.

ULYSSES
(Rising abruptly, angry)

Was that all she used?

EUMAEUS
(Sharply)

It was! Penelope keeps to herself. She's a prisoner in her own room. The men may be masters of your house, but she is still your wife.

ULYSSES
(More subdued; still bitter)

All right, all right... So I come home, and I find eleven men living in my house. That's just the welcome I wanted.

EUMAEUS

You're lucky. There used to be more of them. Nearly a hundred at one time.

ULYSSES

What?

EUMAEUS

Sure, sure... Then some got killed—a quarrelsome lot they are. And the cowards gave up, and drifted away. Now there are only eleven. But they are the dangerous ones. There are two, in particular—real bastards they are... The women seem to like them, though.

ULYSSES

Just how young are they?

EUMAEUS

Younger than you are.

ULYSSES

How do they fight?

EUMAEUS

They can fight, all right. They're strong. Well set-up. Women would call them handsome.

ULYSSES
(Puzzled)

But what keeps them here? I'd imagine that the attractions of Ithaca are a little limited for eleven handsome braggarts.

EUMAEUS

Well—you see—

ULYSSES

I don't. They aren't the type to work the land. Food is short, you said. So what *keeps* them here?

EUMAEUS

They have the idea that one of them is going to marry Penelope and become lord of this island. That's what they are gambling for—power, and a beautiful woman. Isn't that enough to keep them waiting?

ULYSSES

Marry my wife?

EUMAEUS

You're dead, aren't you? That's what brought them here, in the first place.

ULYSSES
(Boiling up)
And who is this lout, this pretentious oaf, who's going to marry my wife?

EUMAEUS

She will decide.

ULYSSES
(Exploding)
Penelope will *choose*?

EUMAEUS

That's the agreement. Women have brains, too, you know. She has kept them dangling and bickering and waiting for three years. Don't ask me how she does it, but—

ULYSSES
(Grimly)

I won't.

EUMAEUS

Now, Ulysses—

ULYSSES

Eleven of them...

EUMAEUS

And their servants, of course. They each brought two.

ULYSSES

All men? Can they fight?

EUMAEUS

Constantly. But they wouldn't have much stomach in facing you.
(As ULYSSES *gives a short, bitter laugh)*
No, I'd just worry about their masters, if I were you. Fight them, and the rest will run.

ULYSSES

So that's all I have to do? Fight eleven men.
(He drops the irony, and becomes serious.)
How many can we put up against them?

EUMAEUS

Well—there's me; Telemachus, your son; and Philetius. Of
course, he isn't what he used to be—still feels the wounds he
got in the war. The Trojans tore out his tongue, did you know
that? So he is dumb. But he's faithful. He has stayed here—

ULYSSES

Philetius...so he got home safely, did he? He's a good man in
any fight.—Who else?

EUMAEUS

That's all.

ULYSSES

(Swings round to stare at EUMAEUS*)*
Two old men, and a boy—that's all who are left?

EUMAEUS

But you can handle a sword better than ten men put together!

ULYSSES

That old myth!... We'll need more than our swords.
(He sits down, thoroughly depressed.)
We'll have to put our brains to work, Eumaeus.

EUMAEUS

(Hesitating)

I don't suppose they gave you anything to eat or drink in the village?

(ULYSSES is lost in his worry and dejection.)

That's what you need.

(He hurries into the shack, comes out with a hunk of bread and a small flask of wine, ULYSSES takes them, with a nod, still lost in thought.)

You know the best idea? Now that you're home—

(ULYSSES breaks the bread, and shares it with EUMAEUS.)

—we could all escape. There's a boat in the Bay just below your house. Remember it? Penelope had Philetius keep it in good order.

(ULYSSES looks at him now, but still goes on chewing.)

It takes five men to sail it, but with you as one of the crew, we could manage it. We could all leave—tonight—when it's dark.

ULYSSES

And give up my land and my home to these invaders?

(He drinks from the flask, then passes it over to EUMAEUS.)

Like hell I will.

EUMAEUS

But we could come back—with more men, a small army—

ULYSSES

If no one came to help Penelope, in all these years, they wouldn't come now. Why didn't they come, the damned cowards?

EUMAEUS

They had their own lands to put in order, once they got back from the war. Hey—did you hear what happened to Agamemnon? Got his throat slit in his bath on the day he got home.

(Drinks quickly)

Yes, his wife, Clytemnestra, and her lover took over his palace at Mycenae—

ULYSSES

(Grimly)

Are you trying to warn me that I'll get my throat slit, too?

EUMAEUS

(Shocked)

Penelope isn't like that. She's—

ULYSSES

Sure, sure. Just kept eleven men hanging around for three solid years. Who's the one she is going to marry?

EUMAEUS

Now, look here—

ULYSSES

I think—I think I'd like to talk with my son. Go up to the house, Eumaeus. Find him. Bring him here.

EUMAEUS

Right away?

ULYSSES

Right away. But be careful. Tell no one else that I'm alive. Or that I have come back. No one.

EUMAEUS

Not even Penelope?

ULYSSES
(Softly)

Least of all Penelope.
(He draws his cloak more closely around him, sits brooding, biting the knuckles of his right fist, ignoring EUMAEUS, who leaves, shaking his head. ULYSSES is motionless. Suddenly he strikes his fist on the ground. He speaks in anger.)

You gods in Heaven—do you never give a man any peace?

ATHENA
(Speaking sadly, from the darkness)

Ulysses—have you forgotten me?

ULYSSES
(His anger changing to anguish)

Athena! In the name of Reason!

ATHENA
(Her voice brightening as the light strengthens to show
her more clearly)

That's better! It was I who brought you safely home, don't forget.

ULYSSES

Why should this be my home-coming? Why, *why*?

ATHENA

(Sighing, as she speaks to the audience)

It's always the way. When things go wrong, all you human beings start asking, "Why, why, why?" As if the gods were to blame for your troubles.

(She walks slowly, gracefully, over to ULYSSES.*)*

Look into yourself, Ulysses. Look deeply. Everything changes, nothing stays as it was. That's why the human comedy goes on, and on...

ULYSSES

(Angry again)

It's a joke on me. A bitter, sour-smelling joke.

(He rises.)

I've had enough of it. Old Eumaeus was right—there's no sense in staying. I have my pride.

ATHENA

Your vanity, you mean. Oh, it's badly wounded, I admit. But perhaps it needed a little deflating? What is a cruel joke but just another challenge? And *you* will walk away from it? And call it meaningless?—Then the joke *is* bitter: you'll turn it into tragedy. Ulysses—*listen* to my voice. I'm putting reason into your head. Use it!

ULYSSES

(Takes two steps, hesitates, halts)

And yet, I'll be damned if I'll let other men dictate the shape of my life.

(Instead of leaving, he paces around.)

So, they thought they could challenge me, did they? We'll see about that... We'll see...

(He laughs, briefly, grimly.)

ATHENA

(To the audience)

That wasn't much of a laugh, but he will improve. Yes, our patient is coming out of shock. Emotions under control, heart strong, brain working. Now we'll prescribe a little rest, some concentrated thought, and purge the self-pity right out of him. Really—

*(She begins to leave, passing ULYSSES with a light touch
of farewell on his shoulder, which he can't notice, of
course.)*

if anyone had any complaints in this world, it should be me. I haven't had one free hour to myself, since that frontal lobe was invented.

*(Calls gently back to ULYSSES, who has been staring
thoughtfully into the middle distance ever since her
touch on the shoulder)*

The gods gave you a brain. Use it. Stupidity never did produce a happy ending. Think well, my friend. Don't disappoint me, now. I *hate* tragedy—it's such a waste!

(She laughs and goes out.)

ULYSSES

(Drops back onto the ground at the door of the shack.

31

He resumes the position he had adopted when EUMAEUS
left him, but now his rage has gone. He speaks quietly.)
Penelope, Penelope… And I was so sure of you.
(He shakes his head sadly, then falls into deep thought.
His face is hard and cold. The curtain closes slowly.)

SCENE 2

We are in PENELOPE's *private sitting room, a kind of anteroom to her bedroom, whose massive bronze door lies in the centre of the back wall. Upstage to the left is the window; downstage to the right is the door to the sitting room. On either side of the bronze door stand three low-backed chairs, covered with embroidery in bright wools. Opposite the window, placed dramatically against the right upstage corner of the room, is a large and impressive leather chair. Beside it rest an equally large and impressive shield and spear. The only other furnishings in this room consist of an embroidery frame, a stool, and a small side table (with wools and cutting knife)—all grouped on the left, downstage, as if* PENELOPE *liked to face the leather chair as she worked.*

It is early morning. CLIA, *a white-haired elderly woman, dressed in a dark wool robe, is tidying the room. She is picking up skeins of gaily coloured wool from the floor, laying them on the little side table. She pauses for a moment to look at the embroidery, and shakes her head with a sigh.* AMARYLLIS *enters, a pretty young girl with a saucy air. She is dressed in a yellow robe, and she is carrying a small tray with fruit, wheat cakes, and honey, and a flask of wine.*

AMARYLLIS
(As she enters)
Well, here's breakfast... Is she up yet?
(She nods toward the bronze door, and starts in that direction.)

CLIA
(Dropping everything to intercept AMARYLLIS)
Give me the tray.

AMARYLLIS
Oh, let me take it in. Just once!

CLIA
No one enters that room except me.

AMARYLLIS
(Slyly)
Afraid I'll tell the men downstairs what her bedroom looks like?

CLIA
They'd give a lot to know.

(She carries the tray toward the bedroom door, and
AMARYLLIS *moves quietly over to the embroidery frame.)*

And another thing—When you are talking of the mistress, don't call her "she." Call her Penelope. If you can't keep your own self-respect with those men downstairs, then at least give respect to women who've earned it.

AMARYLLIS

(Examining the embroidery curiously)

It isn't *my* fault that the house is filled with men. I didn't bring them here.

CLIA

You certainly don't object to them living here!

(She looks round as she speaks, and sees AMARYLLIS *touching the embroidery stretched on the frame. She puts down the tray on a chair beside the bronze door, and rushes at the girl.)*

What are you doing now? Out you go! Get on with your work!

AMARYLLIS

All right, all right... Stop pushing! I'm going!

(She moves toward the entrance door.)

You know why you are so bad-tempered in the morning? You never get kissed at night. You're too old to be kissed, that's *your* trouble.

(PENELOPE has entered, closing the bedroom door quietly behind her. She stands there, watching the two maids. She is an extremely beautiful woman in her early thirties. Her dress is a simple grey wool robe.)

AMARYLLIS
(Frightened now, and very subdued)
Good morning, Penelope.

PENELOPE
Good morning, Amaryllis.
(She doesn't move from the bronze door. AMARYLLIS goes out quickly. Then PENELOPE comes forward, slowly. Her voice is calm, almost lifeless.)
Good morning, Clia.

CLIA
Morning.
(She watches PENELOPE worriedly as she wanders around the room.)
That Amaryllis—she's getting too brash.

PENELOPE
So I heard.
(She is now standing at the embroidery frame, looking at it gloomily.)

CLIA
You heard everything?

PENELOPE
It wasn't difficult.
(She gives a short, bitter laugh.)
So we are too old, are we? *That's* our trouble?

CLIA

Now, now... Here's your breakfast. Where will you have it? At the window?
> *(She lays the tray, as she speaks, on the side table, and*
> *pulls it nearer to the window.)*

Look, it's a fine bright morning. Good sailing weather, Penelope.

PENELOPE

Except, there isn't any ship.

CLIA

Why, there are a lot of ships down in the harbour this morning. I saw three fishing boats headed straight for this island, even before the sun came rising out of the sea.

PENELOPE
> *(Turning her back on the window)*

But not the ship bringing my husband.

CLIA

Ulysses could have been on one of those boats!

PENELOPE
> *(Suddenly coming to life as she faces* CLIA)

You've told me that too often. This is the last morning you are to talk of ships. The *last* morning, d'you hear?

CLIA

Penelope! You aren't giving up hope?

PENELOPE
(Dejected)

I—I don't know...

*(She sits down on the stool in front of the embroidery
frame. Her body droops.)*

CLIA

But you *can't* give up hope!

PENELOPE

It's hope that has given me up.

CLIA

But hope is life...

PENELOPE

And what kind of life do I have?

CLIA

You're young—

PENELOPE

Too old to be kissed, according to Amaryllis.

CLIA

You're still beautiful—

PENELOPE
(Wryly)

Still? Thank you...

CLIA

My, you've had a bad night, haven't you? Come on. Eat something and you'll feel much better. Look, here's clover honey—you always liked that—and wheat cakes.

(She fusses with the tray.)

I can remember the first morning I ever served you breakfast in this room... Your hair was as gold as the sun streaming in that window.

PENELOPE

(Sitting in front of the breakfast tray, but still not touching it)

At least, the sun hasn't changed.

CLIA

(Quickly)

Just fifteen you were, then. Slender as a willow branch. Eyes as blue as a bed of iris.

PENELOPE

(Almost smiling)

That was the morning I awoke saying, "Why, I'm a grown-up woman! I'm *old*, at last!"

(She shakes her head in amusement.)

CLIA

That was the morning you got honey all over your fingers, and you licked them when you thought Ulysses wasn't looking. But he was noticing everything you did—sitting over in that chair, he was—

(She points to the large chair, upstage right.)
and he let out a roar of laughter. Remember how he used to laugh?

PENELOPE

Don't... Don't!

CLIA

And you looked up at him, and the colour spread over your cheeks, and you began to laugh, too. Then I knew you were the right wife for Ulysses.

PENELOPE
(Rising abruptly)

Stop it, Clia, stop it!
(She begins to pace around the room.)
So you knew I was the right wife for Ulysses! How can I be *any* kind of wife if I have no husband?

CLIA

Now, now—

PENELOPE

Seventeen years of waiting... Seventeen years since he went off to fight.

CLIA

I know, I know... It was a long war.

PENELOPE

Ten years long. Where's your arithmetic, Clia? Ten from seventeen leaves a lot of waiting.

(Her anger changes to fear.)

Doesn't Ulysses ever want to see our island again? Or his son? Or me?

(She begins to weep.)

CLIA

(Comforting PENELOPE*)*

Ulysses *will* come home. Put that fear out of your mind. He will come back—just wait and see.

PENELOPE

I've waited and waited, and what have I seen? Ship after ship sailing into harbour, and still no Ulysses. He doesn't want to come back, Clia.

CLIA

Now, you aren't being fair. Troy is a far journey from Ithaca.

PENELOPE

Not seven years far!

CLIA

But we live on an island. We've been stormbound for the worst seven winters, one right after another, that *I*'ve ever seen.

PENELOPE

Seven winters had seven summers.

CLIA

(Her voice sharpening)

Will you listen to me?

PENELOPE

I've always listened to you. That's been part of my trouble.

CLIA

Your trouble is that you've been thinking too much about yourself and too little about Ulysses.

PENELOPE

(Too hurt to be angry)

Oh, Clia!

CLIA

(More gently)

Well, in this last week you certainly have. I've been watching you—sitting here, boiling up like a volcano. Ulysses has had his share of problems, don't forget.

PENELOPE

(Miserable, in a low voice)

What colour of hair did they have?

CLIA

(Angry again)

Shipping was scarce after the war. It still is. All the veterans had trouble finding transportation.

PENELOPE

But they came home, didn't they? They're home now.

CLIA
(Quietly)

Not all of them.

PENELOPE
(Chastened)

Some will never come back... But at least, their women know that. They know the worst. I don't. I know *nothing*. You can't go on living with nothing, Clia.

CLIA
(Her anger increasing with her worry)

All right, I'll give you something to live with! I've been trying to keep the news from you, but—
(She breaks off, upset. As her control weakens, PENELOPE becomes strong, calm, alert.)

PENELOPE

What is it, Clia? More trouble with our unwanted guests?

CLIA

Trouble? Disaster! Those men downstairs—they've taken over your house, they've bullied and threatened and thieved—

PENELOPE

Now, Clia, stop upsetting yourself. It won't help us deal with those men, I assure you. Look, I'll make a bargain with you—

(She sits down before the breakfast tray.)
I'll eat some breakfast if you'll tell me *quietly* just what is the
trouble now.

    (She pours some wine in a goblet, waters it, and begins
    to sip. Slowly, though. And she eats very little. She is
    only making the pretence to please CLIA.*)*

Well?

CLIA

(Recovering herself, wiping her eyes, shaking her head
in amazement)
Are you never afraid of them, Penelope?

PENELOPE

Constantly. Does that make you feel any better?

CLIA

I couldn't feel worse. We've got to *do* something, Penelope.

PENELOPE

Do? What can we do, except play for time and use our wits?

CLIA

Do you know how much food we have left? Enough for two
days. The fields haven't been ploughed. The barns are empty.
Summer is here, but there's nothing growing—except grass
and weeds.

PENELOPE

Last spring, we ploughed the fields. And last fall, we harvested.
What did we get?—Another winter of these men.

CLIA

They're drunk from morning till night.

PENELOPE

Then the cellars will soon be as empty as the barns. Good.

CLIA

You mean—you planned it this way? But you've left *us* with
nothing. Our cattle and sheep have been killed and eaten.
There's hardly a deer left in all our forests, we've nothing, I tell
you, nothing!

PENELOPE

Except ourselves. You are still alive, Clia. So is Telemachus, so
is the rest of the household. Once the men have gone, we can
work. We can restore everything. We can live on fish from the
sea, if necessary. But meanwhile, the important thing is that we
are intact.

CLIA

Intact? You weren't referring to the maids, were you? You
should go down into the Hall more often instead of sitting up
here, and see how the girls are behaving.

PENELOPE

It's wiser to stay here, Clia. The less I'm seen, the better.

CLIA

There's no decency left. No discipline. I warned you when you gave the girls their freedom—

PENELOPE

I'll have no slaves in my house!

CLIA
(Bitterly)

That's right, give them their freedom, give them a home, and what do *you* get? Loyalty? Huh! Collaborators, that's what they are. A whipping, that's what they need; and their heads shaved. Perhaps that would put some morals into their manners.

PENELOPE

Clia, when you were young, very young, did you never do foolish, thoughtless—no, I don't suppose you ever did.
(She smiles, affectionately, sadly.)
But put the blame where it first belongs. Put it on the men.

CLIA

If they'd only *leave*! I'd starve with pleasure, and work with fury, if only they'd leave and take the girls with them.

PENELOPE

And what would happen to the girls?
*(She pushes away the breakfast tray, and rises to walk
slowly over to the embroidery frame.)*
Abandoned in some filthy brothel in a harbour slum. Besides—
(She looks at the embroidery.)

the men are playing for higher stakes than just a pretty girl. They want land, and the title to this house. They want power over all the island of Ithaca. If they can persuade me to marry one of them, they will have that power. Forever. Legally.

CLIA

Legally! Since when have they paid any attention to the law?

PENELOPE

(Sitting down at the frame, and beginning to thread a needle with wool)

But they know that *other* men pay heed to the law.

CLIA

Twisters, liars, cheats! They say they're in love with you, they only want to protect you.

(PENELOPE bends her head, pretending to be absorbed in her work.)

Huh! Just look at the way they play around with your maids!

PENELOPE

That's to punish me, Clia, for taking so little notice of them. Don't you think I hear the laughter and singing when I'm up here at night, alone?

(She points to the bedroom door, almost angrily.)

CLIA

(Shocked)

Penelope! You can't envy that kind of laughing and singing? Penelope—answer me!

PENELOPE

Don't be silly.

CLIA

That's no answer.

PENELOPE
(Suddenly angry)

Clia, I've done my best to get rid of these men. When they came here first—

CLIA

I knew they were up to no good, the moment I saw them.

PENELOPE

We don't all have your brilliant hindsight, Clia... I'm sorry... We've plenty of troubles without bickering like this between ourselves. You'll just have to believe me, Clia! I've done my best.
(She sighs and her head droops.)

CLIA

Oh, you haven't done too badly, considering.

PENELOPE
(Looking up quickly)

Considering what?

CLIA

Now, don't go taking offence again! I'm not criticising you. You've done remarkably well. Considering.

*(*PENELOPE *looks at her indignantly.)*
Considering you were young, and lonely. It was good, wasn't it, to hear a man's voice, a man's footsteps once more?

PENELOPE

You didn't object, either, did you?

CLIA

I'm not blaming you. Of course they were only a bit of a nuisance at first. Yes, a pleasant, flattering kind of nuisance.

PENELOPE

Flattering?

CLIA

All that talk of wanting to marry you! Stuff and nonsense!

PENELOPE
(Sarcastically)
Ridiculous! No man could ever possibly want to marry *me*!

CLIA

Ah-hah! Did I throw some salt on a small wound? Then good! It'll heal more cleanly. An open wound's a dangerous thing with so much infection around.
(She suddenly touches PENELOPE *on the shoulder and speaks gently.)*
Keep on fighting those men, Penelope. You've done better than most.

PENELOPE

(Covers her eyes with her hands for a moment)

Clia, have you ever watched a fox being chased by a pack of wild dogs?... It twists and turns, it uses all its cunning, all its speed, all its strength. And then suddenly it stops. It stops and faces them. Do you know what the fox is thinking then, Clia?

CLIA

It's just out of breath, that's all.

PENELOPE

It suddenly knows that courage is not enough.

CLIA

Nonsense! What does anyone need except courage?

PENELOPE

My fox needs twenty other foxes standing beside it—with teeth twice as long as any dog's.

(She tries to laugh.)

CLIA

(Moving to the window)

Just wait! Just wait until Ulysses comes home!

(She stares out of the window.)

He'll show those parasites what it's like to deal with a man for a change. That's the whole trouble with this house—

PENELOPE

Come away from the window, Clia. Stop thinking about ships.

CLIA

—we're nothing but a handful of women, and a young boy, and Philetius, who can't even talk, and old Eumaeus, who's good for nothing except pig-keeping.

(She sees something outside.)

Why, he isn't even doing that! There he is, dawdling about. Eumaeus!

(She raises her voice.)

What are you doing here? Get back to your meadow and look after the chickens—don't you know we've got thieves around?

(She turns away from the window, and derisive catcalls come from the distance.)

The thieves didn't like my frankness. They must be getting up. It's early for them, isn't it?

PENELOPE

Perhaps they—

(She shrugs her shoulders.)

Perhaps—if—but—maybe... I've lived too long with these words.

(She breaks a strand of wool angrily.)

CLIA

(Coming to pick up a fallen skein of wool)

You're getting *awfully* near the end of that embroidery. Better rip some more out again. Here!

(She lifts a knife lying beside the wools on the side table, and hands it to PENELOPE, *who takes it, but looks at* CLIA *and hesitates.)*

Go on! Now's a good time, when none of the maids can watch.

PENELOPE

I've been ripping it out for weeks. Oh, Clia, I just can't rip out much more, without the whole thing coming to pieces.

CLIA

Rip it out! You mustn't finish that embroidery.

PENELOPE

But I pledged my word.
(She sighs and begins to unpick the stitches carefully.)

CLIA

Whatever made you give the men such a stupid promise?

PENELOPE

Stupid? It was your idea. Promise them anything, you told me, as long as you keep them quiet until Ulysses gets home. Tell them you need time to make up your mind which one you'll choose for a husband—that's what you said. All right. I told them. I told them I'd choose one of them when I finished embroidering a set of seven chair covers. Wasn't that your idea?

CLIA

But why did you ever have to take a solemn oath—and in Athena's temple, too? A promise is one thing but an oath is something else. I never told you to do that. And why choose Athena? Of all the gods, she gets maddest when her name is taken in vain. She'll follow a perjurer right to his grave, and beyond that, too.

PENELOPE

I know that. So do the men downstairs. They'd have broken their bargain long ago, if they weren't afraid of Athena.

(She begins to rip out some more stitches, and jabs her finger. She exclaims and puts it to her mouth; she looks in dismay at the embroidery.)

Heavens! This is an awful mess... If anyone who knows a thing about embroidery ever sees this—then I'm going to be found out.

(She sighs.)

If the men realise I've been tricking them—

CLIA

Amaryllis—this morning—*she* was looking at it.

PENELOPE

Amaryllis? Oh no, Clia. Amaryllis wouldn't betray me.

CLIA

Wouldn't she?

PENELOPE

But she has no reason to betray—

CLIA

And wouldn't she like to become mistress of this house? That's reason enough.

PENELOPE

(Shocked)

I don't believe you trust anyone in this world! Except Ulysses. He can do no wrong in your eyes. All right, let me ask you a question: *why* isn't he here? Why isn't he here to take charge and free us from all these dangers and troubles and fears? Why? Why?

CLIA

Here we go again. You *have* had a bad night.
> *(There's the sound of horsemen in the distance.* CLIA *moves quickly over to the window. Men's voices come faintly, then die away. So does the sound of the horses' hoofs.)*

Are they going out hunting, d'you think? They must have taken the back road.
> *(She suddenly looks down into the courtyard, plants her hands on her hips.)*

Well!—And who do you think is still around? Eumaeus. Wasting time, as usual.

PENELOPE
(Snipping carefully)

Who isn't?

CLIA

And he's got hold of your son. Talking like conspirators, they are. Eumaeus!
> *(*PENELOPE *looks up, quickly.)*

CLIA
(Shouting now)

Eumaeus! Get back to your work, do you hear me?

(To PENELOPE*)*

My, he looked up at me as if he were scared.

PENELOPE

(Rising)

Is something wrong?

CLIA

(Turning away from the window, as PENELOPE *starts
toward her and then stops)*

They are out of sight now. He pulled Telemachus around the
corner of the house. What are they hiding, I'd like to know?

(The two women stare at each other.)

I've warned you before about Eumaeus—

PENELOPE

Go down to them, Clia. And send Eumaeus here.

CLIA

Send that pig-keeper up here—into your room?

PENELOPE

I want to see him.

CLIA

Why?

PENELOPE

...Just a sudden fear... That's all.

CLIA

Yes, I've warned you. Eumaeus has some very odd ideas. Why, the girls won't even go near his hut. You've let Telemachus visit him too often.

PENELOPE

Eumaeus wouldn't harm any son of Ulysses. And the boy has to have some man to talk to. We can't hold on to him, Clia. If we do—we lose him forever.

CLIA

Is *that* what's been troubling you this morning? No Ulysses, and soon, no Telemachus. Is that what's worrying you?
(She comes forward and puts her arm around PENELOPE.)

PENELOPE
(Slowly)
I'm not worried... I'm frightened.
(She starts to pace around the room.)
If Ulysses *ever* does come home, will it be too late? Too late for Telemachus? Too late for me? And if he comes home, shall I know him? Will he know me? Or have I been waiting for a stranger, for someone so altered that he won't be in love with me any more?
(She halts and faces a very silent CLIA.)
I'm frightened, Clia!

CLIA
(Gathering her words slowly)
Now that's stupid... Of course you'll know him. Ulysses is

Ulysses. He's strong, clever, brave—

PENELOPE

Stop it! You aren't Homer. Leave the adjectives to him. Now, go and find Eumaeus. And you can send Telemachus here, too. He hasn't paid me a visit for three whole days.

CLIA

Don't be hard on the boy. He's only angry because the men have been behaving worse and worse. And he feels helpless—he knows he's too young to fight even one of them. But that may not stop him from trying. One thing is certain, if the men don't leave here soon, there will be trouble. There will be red blood flowing all over this house.

PENELOPE

Is *that* what he is plotting with old Eumaeus? Oh, no! In Heaven's name, go and get them—
(*As* CLIA *opens the door, there are sounds of men arguing; laughter; and a delighted squeal from a girl.* PENELOPE *covers her ears, and turns her back on the door. A boy of about seventeen passes* CLIA *as she is just about to leave. This is* TELEMACHUS; *he is thin and gangling, white-faced, not very handsome as yet. He is dressed in a simple tunic and wears a large knife at his waist which he fingers proudly from time to time.* CLIA *whispers a quick warning to him and points to* PENELOPE'S *back. Then she goes out.*)

TELEMACHUS

Hello, Mother. I was just coming to see you.

(He tries to hide his cheerfulness, but there is repressed
excitement in his voice as he rushes on. PENELOPE *turns*
to look at him with surprise.)

It's a grand day, isn't it? I think I'll go fishing down by the meadows. Eumaeus has made me a new rod. It's waiting for me in his hut. I'll go and get it, if you don't mind.

*(*PENELOPE *is now staring at him.)*

Just didn't want to worry you about where I was. Well—see you later!

(He hesitates nervously, grins, and turns to leave.)

PENELOPE

Telemachus! I want to see you *now.*

TELEMACHUS

(Turning back to PENELOPE, *slowly, unwillingly)*
But I'm going fishing—

PENELOPE

I want to talk to you.

TELEMACHUS

Couldn't it wait? I mean, this is kind of important. If I don't start before the sun is bright, then I'll never catch *anything.*

PENELOPE

The sun only rose three hours ago. It has a long way to travel before it's too bright for fishing. What's wrong, Telemachus?

TELEMACHUS

Wrong?

PENELOPE

You heard me.

TELEMACHUS

Nothing's *wrong*.

PENELOPE

Then stop hovering around that door. And sit down. No—that's your father's chair. You know the rule.

TELEMACHUS

Couldn't I sit in it once, before he gets home?

PENELOPE

*(Smiling as she shakes her head and gestures him away
from* ULYSSES' *chair)*

You're just like Clia, aren't you?

TELEMACHUS

(Indignant)

Me? Like Clia?

PENELOPE

You are both so sure that Ulysses will come home.

TELEMACHUS

He will.

PENELOPE

(Watching him carefully)

Have you heard any news? Do you know something that I don't know?

TELEMACHUS

Now, Mother, what gave you that idea?

PENELOPE

You're looking so annoyingly cheerful, that's why.

TELEMACHUS

Well—you see—I just thought you *wanted* me to be more cheerful. Last time I saw you, you tore into me because I was sulking. That's the word you used.

PENELOPE

Perhaps it was. But I never "tore into you" in my whole life.

TELEMACHUS

(Appeasingly)

All right.

PENELOPE

It seems to me I'm getting my own way awfully easily, this morning.

TELEMACHUS

I'm just *trying* to *please* you. Oh, Jupiter!

PENELOPE

Now, careful! Don't call on the gods unless you want their help. They don't like it. Then when you really need them, you can call and call but they won't answer. I've told you that before.

TELEMACHUS
(Patiently)

Yes, Mother.

PENELOPE

Oh darling, don't make me sound as if I were a general or something. I don't order you around: I'm just—I'm just trying to teach you the real facts of life. It's so *hard* for a woman to be a father!
(She tries to laugh.)
Where's Eumaeus, I wonder? I sent Clia to fetch him.

TELEMACHUS

I bet she's giving him a bath, first. He smells a bit high.
(He becomes suddenly worried.)
His shack is awful. Not the kind of place *you'd* want to visit.

PENELOPE
(Surprised and amused)

I wasn't thinking of paying old Eumaeus a visit in his shack.
(She watches TELEMACHUS' *relief.)*
But what do you find so interesting there?

TELEMACHUS

Nothing. Nothing. Except Eumaeus. It's good to have a man to talk to. There's only women in this house—or Philetius over at the stable, and he's dumb. It really is pretty lonely here.

PENELOPE

Yes, it's lonely… But I hope all the travelling you did last year hasn't unsettled you.

TELEMACHUS

But you said travelling abroad was good for my education.

PENELOPE

If it doesn't make you discontented with home.

TELEMACHUS

When Father was here, it wasn't lonely. Was it?

(PENELOPE *shakes her head.*)

TELEMACHUS

No, there were plenty of *real* men around then. All *his* men. They were good fighters and hunters, weren't they?

PENELOPE

And good farmers, too. They could plough a straight furrow and raise a fine crop.

TELEMACHUS

Now, Mother, don't start hinting again. You're always giving double meanings to everything.

PENELOPE

Well, someone has got to teach you to keep a balance. You don't want to grow up to be like those men downstairs, do you?

TELEMACHUS

Mother!

PENELOPE

Life isn't all hunting or fighting, or trying to live at someone else's expense. There are houses to be built, and people to be fed and clothed. There are children to be raised; and music to be made; and poetry to be sung.

TELEMACHUS
(Fingering the knife at his belt)
My father was a hunter. A hunter and a soldier.

PENELOPE

Ulysses was many things. He was the son of a prince, but he came here and settled this land and founded his own family. He was a good farmer, too. He could plough the straightest furrow—
(She pauses, looks slyly at TELEMACHUS, *adds softly)*
Yes, he was ploughing, on the day the draft board came to get him.

TELEMACHUS

The draft board? Why, Mother, you *know* Father volunteered the day the Trojan War broke out. Why, he was the best fighter in the whole army!

PENELOPE

I think so... But he was also a very clever man.

TELEMACHUS

That's why the army put him in Intelligence. I *know* all that! Why, he invented the Trojan Horse. He *won* the war!

PENELOPE

Yes, once he was in the army, he fought; and he fought well.

TELEMACHUS

I don't like the way you say that.

PENELOPE

It may be that your knowledge is just a little one-sided. It seems that Clia and I haven't given you a very balanced picture of your father. It's about time you admired him for the way he could plough a field as well as for the way he could capture a city with a wooden horse.

TELEMACHUS
(Disgusted)

Plough a field!

PENELOPE
(Sharply)

And build a house. Who built this house? Your father, working with his men. Who cleared the forests and made fields out of wilderness? Who sowed the crops and planted the vines?

TELEMACHUS

And fought the brigands, *and* hunted. He killed a wild boar with *this* knife, all by himself, when he was my age. And he got wounded, too—the boar's tusk slit his leg—

(*He scores his own leg, from below to above his knee.*)

just there, and left a scar to this day.

PENELOPE

Darling, might I remind you I've been listening to Clia's stories about Ulysses longer than you have? And considering you were three months old when you last saw your father, it's possible that some incidents may have escaped you.

TELEMACHUS

Oh, now, Mother! You don't have to go all stiff-starched... I'm sorry... Look, I'll even listen to what you were going to tell me about the draft board.

PENELOPE

I don't think I shall tell you.

TELEMACHUS

I *said* I was sorry.

PENELOPE

Perhaps you aren't old enough to understand. When you are a man, you can be told. But now, you only want to hear the things you wish to believe.

TELEMACHUS

But I *want* to hear this story. *Please...*

PENELOPE

Well, if you must hear it… We'll begin with Helen, who started all our troubles anyway. She left her husband and ran away with Paris—

TELEMACHUS

(Impatiently)

—to Troy. I know all the dates and everything about *that*. Tell me about Father!

PENELOPE

He said that if Helen preferred Paris to her husband, then it was none of our business.

TELEMACHUS

But—

PENELOPE

Yes, I know. People went around saying it was "a Trojan insult to Greek womanhood"; although, personally, I never felt in the least insulted. I don't think any other woman did, either.

TELEMACHUS

But, we had to go and get Helen back.

PENELOPE

Very flattering for Helen, wasn't it?

TELEMACHUS

Now, Mother, that isn't—

PENELOPE

Yes, I'm bitter. And why not?

TELEMACHUS

I don't like you that way; Father wouldn't, either.

PENELOPE

(Chastened, half-smiling)

You know what? You're very good for me... But I still think it was the stupidest reason for a war that ever was. Why, Helen didn't even want to come back to her husband. All right, all right, Telemachus. Don't look at me as if I were a green-eyed cat with long claws. I'm just putting you in the picture, or else you'll *never* understand about the draft board.

TELEMACHUS

(Tries to look wise, nods understandingly, and then— as he suddenly notices the uneaten cakes and honey— becomes his age again)

Oh! Cakes and honey! Don't you want them? Are you sure?

(PENELOPE shakes her head, smiling, as TELEMACHUS reaches for the cakes.)

All right—Father was drafted. Then what?

PENELOPE

He got an exemption because he happened to marry me.

(TELEMACHUS stops eating for a moment and looks at her.)

Then the draft was extended. To include all married men who had no children. But *you* were born. So, we got another exemption.

(TELEMACHUS, who has started to eat again, pauses.)

Then, a little later, all men had to go into the army.

TELEMACHUS

And Father went off to the war.

PENELOPE

No… You see, he hadn't been feeling too well. So he applied for another exemption. As a P.N., this time.

TELEMACHUS

P.N.?

PENELOPE

Psychoneurotic, darling… *You* know…
(She taps her forehead lightly.)

TELEMACHUS

Father?

PENELOPE

Don't worry—and finish the cake; it's the last we'll see for some time—your father wasn't crazy, not one bit. He was the sanest man I ever knew.

TELEMACHUS

Then why a P.N.? He wasn't a coward!

PENELOPE
(Angry)

If he had been a coward, would I tell you all this? No, I'd be hiding it from you, covering it up. Ulysses wasn't a coward.

But he was stubborn. And he didn't want to go off and fight for good old Helen or any other runaway wife.

TELEMACHUS
(Relieved, and finishing the cake with pleasure)
He *was* clever, wasn't he?

PENELOPE
And so was the draft board. When he wouldn't go to them, they came to him.

TELEMACHUS
They travelled all the way to this island? Boy! That was something!

PENELOPE
When they arrived, Ulysses was working in the big field. And I was standing, with you in my arms, watching him as he ploughed. Some of the draft board he knew, but he looked at them blankly, as if he saw straight through them; no smile, no expression; and he went on ploughing, like a sleepwalker. Back and forward, back and forward, along the straight furrows. "Doesn't he know anyone?" one of his old friends said to me. And I looked at him with tears in my eyes for an answer. But the chairman of the draft board—later, he got killed in the war; wasn't that too bad?—anyway, he suddenly lifted you right out of my arms, carried you across the furrows, and laid you down on the earth just in front of Ulysses. Ulysses paused, and swerved, and the sharp edge of the ploughshare missed you... That is how they knew he was sane. And Ulysses knew he was beaten. He left the plough, and picked you up, and brought you back to me. He went away, that day.

(Her voice falters, and she can't go on.)

TELEMACHUS
(Slowly, terribly serious)

I'm not sure if I understand that story. But one thing's sure—he loved me. Didn't he? He loved me, even if I wasn't old enough to know who he was. And what's more, he was a hero when he did start fighting. He was a hero, wasn't he?

PENELOPE

They say he was the greatest of them all. So that makes him all the braver, because he did not want to fight in *that* war.

TELEMACHUS

I'm not sure I understand that, either. I've a lot of thinking to do...

PENELOPE

Then I've given you a good lesson, today. School's over; class dismissed.
(Laughing, now)
What about going down to Eumaeus' shack and picking up the fishing rod? Catch me a speckled trout, Telemachus. I'll eat it for supper.
(She blows a kiss as TELEMACHUS *opens the door. There are sounds of men's voices. He turns back, quickly, closing the door.)*

TELEMACHUS

I forgot! They're packing up.

PENELOPE

...*The men*? Why didn't you tell me before this?

TELEMACHUS

I meant to—I just forgot—somehow. They sent off their servants this morning. Didn't you hear them riding away?

PENELOPE

You forgot! Or were you too busy thinking about something else? Leaving... Or is this a trick? They could pretend *to each other* that they were leaving and then come back singly. That would be far more dangerous for us. Together, they are a check on each other. Singly—

TELEMACHUS

I'd kill them. I could manage them singly.

PENELOPE

No, you couldn't. In another year or two, yes. But not now.

TELEMACHUS

I have this knife. And I've some weapons hidden. And then I've got Father's Great Bow—the one hanging on the wall downstairs. You know what? The men have never seen one of those big bows. They look at it every day and think it's an old ox yoke or something.
(He loves this.)
But when no one was in the Hall, I've lifted the bow down.
(PENELOPE *looks startled.*)

Yes, I know it takes strength, so I'm stronger than you think. I bet I can string it, too.

PENELOPE

Not even those men downstairs could bend that bow, Telemachus. It takes years of practice. Years. Only Ulysses could.

> *(She puts out a hand and touches his shoulder gently,*
> *as if to cheer him up.)*

TELEMACHUS

Don't worry! We'll take care of them somehow.

PENELOPE

We? I shan't be much use in a fight.

TELEMACHUS

I said don't worry. They won't last long now, one way or the other.

PENELOPE

Why, you aren't afraid of them any more.

> *(She looks at him, puzzled. Then the door opens, letting*
> *in the usual hubbub from the distance and* CLIA *enters*
> *with* EUMAEUS *shambling after her. He is not entirely*
> *repulsive. He has been very handsome in his youth.*
> *He is wearing a blanket around him, which keeps*
> *shifting out of place. He keeps pulling at it, and—at*
> *the moment—is in one of his savage moods. He keeps*
> *looking at* CLIA, *and mutters to himself.)*

CLIA

Well, now, isn't that a nice family picture? And what's this we've strapped to our waist? Your father's hunting knife?

TELEMACHUS
(Drawing himself up and slipping away from PENELOPE*)*
How do I look?
(He squares his shoulders, and puts one hand on the knife.)

CLIA
The living image of your father.

PENELOPE
(Softly)
Oh, Clia!

TELEMACHUS
(Swinging round to face PENELOPE*)*
Don't I look like him? When he was my age?

PENELOPE
I—I didn't know Ulysses when he was seventeen.

TELEMACHUS
But if I don't *look* like him, how will he know me?
(He glances in embarrassment at EUMAEUS, *who is standing quite still and expressionless at this moment.)*
I mean—*if* he comes back.

CLIA

He'll know you at once. Besides, you're wearing his knife, aren't you?

PENELOPE
(Speaking quickly, as she looks out of the window)
The sun is reaching high into the sky, Telemachus.

TELEMACHUS

Oh yes—the sun—well, I'd better be leaving.
(He starts to go out, passing EUMAEUS.)
See you soon?
(He looks quickly back at his mother, who pretends to be studying the embroidery on its frame. CLIA has noticed nothing wrong.)

EUMAEUS

As soon as Clia gives me back my clothes. You go ahead. Had a nice chat with your mother?

TELEMACHUS

Yes. Yes—just a nice chat.
(They exchange a small reassuring sign, TELEMACHUS leaves, his step eager, calling over his shoulder to his mother)
Good-bye now!
(He closes the door with a decided bang.)

PENELOPE

It's all right, Eumaeus. You can relax. He gave nothing away.

(EUMAEUS, and CLIA, too, turn to stare at her. She goes on, crisply, ignoring their looks.)

Clia, I hear that the men are leaving. Is it true?

CLIA

Some are packing, some are squabbling about what they'll take with them.

PENELOPE

Then, why aren't you downstairs, keeping an eye on them?

CLIA

And leave you alone with him?
(She points in horror to EUMAEUS.)

EUMAEUS

You took my tunic away from me, woman—

CLIA

And filthy it was.

EUMAEUS

And you forced me into a bath, and you scrubbed my body, and laughed at me—you and the other maids.

CLIA

Well, you hardly came up to our expectations, after all the grand tales you've spread about yourself.

EUMAEUS

And you made me wear this shroud, and didn't give me a pin to hold it together.

(He has to clutch it suddenly to keep it from slipping.)

Isn't that indignity enough, without pointing that long thin claw at me?

PENELOPE

Clia, please go.

EUMAEUS

And congratulate yourself that, today, you scrubbed the back of a prince.

CLIA

Prince! You're a swine of a swineherd. Your mother was a sow, your father a hog. And now you fondle a pig on your filthy pallet of straw and call him brother.

PENELOPE

Clia!

(CLIA stamps out angrily. PENELOPE looks away for a moment, and then turns to greet EUMAEUS as if he had just entered the room, and all those last minutes were wiped out.)

I'm so glad you came to see me. You're looking very smart—is this a new style in tunics?

EUMAEUS

(Recovering himself from CLIA's attack)

Perhaps I'll start a new fashion.

(He looks down at the length of the blanket.)
Not every man's legs are handsome enough for the short tunic.
Or would it be a pity to hide the handsome legs? How could a
woman then know what she's getting?

PENELOPE
(Amused)
Eumaeus, you can't shock me. So don't waste the strength
you've got left.
*(EUMAEUS grins, and tries to bow, but is hindered by the
blanket. It is still unwinding.)*

EUMAEUS
(Tugging the blanket back in place)
Sweet suffering Jupiter!

PENELOPE
(Watching him)
You're nervous, Eumaeus. You're just a little afraid of me,
today. Why? What are you hiding?

EUMAEUS
Hiding? Nothing, Penelope—
*(He opens his arms; the blanket starts unwinding, and
he clutches it again.)*
Nothing except myself.

PENELOPE
(Suddenly serious)
If you want to lie to me, I suppose you can. I've no claim on

your loyalty—I've only fed you and given you a job so that you could at least earn an honest living.

EUMAEUS

It was Ulysses who gave me that.

PENELOPE
(Angry)

And who has kept you in it? The villagers wanted you driven away. You know that.

EUMAEUS

Yes, they'd have driven me away, all right. But they never offered to chase away those young toughs downstairs, did they? No, they might have been hurt doing that!

PENELOPE

Don't sidetrack me, Eumaeus. The village has been terrorised too, and you know it… I'm angry with you. You've betrayed my trust.

EUMAEUS

I've never done that!

PENELOPE

You've taught my son—

EUMAEUS

No, never! I've taught him nothing. Except what I've become. Once, I was a prince, and look at me now… Women, wine, and dice. That's a sobering lesson for any lad. And that's all I've taught him. I swear it, Penelope!

PENELOPE

You've taught him to deceive me! Something has happened this morning. He knows. You know. And you are both hiding it from me.

EUMAEUS
(Relieved)

We're hiding nothing, nothing to worry about.

PENELOPE

You're lying to me, Eumaeus. And even with all your years of practice, you aren't doing it very well. What do you think I am? A complete fool? That story about a fishing rod! Why, only three days ago, he was complaining that there were no fish left in our streams.

(EUMAEUS' ugly face is lined with worry.)

Why are you sending him to your hut? Why is he so eager to go? Why, Eumaeus, *why*?

(EUMAEUS shrugs his shoulders.)

There's only *one* person in this world who could make you keep silent like this. And that's Ulysses. Is it *Ulysses* who waits in your hut?

EUMAEUS

I—I—There's no one in the hut, except an old beggar who needed a place to rest.

PENELOPE

(Standing over the hapless EUMAEUS, *who tries to avoid her eyes)*

A beggar… A beggar?… It couldn't be. Or is it? Is it Ulysses?

(Her voice rises with joy and amazement. She claps her hands, then she turns back to EUMAEUS, *her voice low, intense.)*

Oh, Eumaeus—you wouldn't lie to me about this? Oh, Eumaeus, you wouldn't…

EUMAEUS

(Frightened)

I said *nothing* about Ulysses!

PENELOPE

No… You didn't, did you? You are not supposed to talk about him? Is that it?

EUMAEUS

I—I—

PENELOPE

The truth, Eumaeus! Or I'll go down to your hut, myself.

EUMAEUS

But the men would follow you—

PENELOPE

Why worry about that, if they'll only find a poor old beggar? Or is it Ulysses they'll find?

(She relents as she sees how miserable EUMAEUS *is. She calms her voice.)*

All right. Let's put it this way. Penelope has been making wild guesses. How wild are they?

(She waits tensely, EUMAEUS *stares unhappily at the ground.)*

I only asked a question about Penelope. Is she wrong in her guesses? *Is* she?

EUMAEUS

No.

PENELOPE

(In sudden joy)

Oh! Dear Athena, kind, sweet Goddess of Reason—you've won, you've won. You've brought him home.

(Almost weeping)

Thank you, thank you.

EUMAEUS

And I'm a dead man before sunset—for answering a question that only dealt with Penelope.

PENELOPE

No, I'll keep this secret, too... But why didn't Ulysses come here? Why all this mystery?

(She is suddenly hurt.)

If this is supposed to be a joke, it isn't funny one bit.

EUMAEUS

If Ulysses had returned—now I'm not saying he did—*if* he had returned, *if* he had heard that a lot of men were in possession here, and *if* he was alone, then what would you expect him to do?

PENELOPE
(Shocked)

He's alone?

EUMAEUS

Now I only said that if he *were* to return, he might be—

PENELOPE

How can he drive out eleven men, by himself?
(She has a sudden idea, begins to smile.)
He must have a plan... Yes, that's it. He's planning something.

EUMAEUS

Why bother? They are leaving, aren't they? That will save him a lot of trouble.

PENELOPE

Yes, it would, wouldn't it?
(Annoyed)
Really! He decides to come back at last, and he expects to walk in here and find everything perfectly normal. Why, he could never even guess the trouble *we've* had.
(Angry, now)
He might even begin to think my story was just the usual female exaggeration!

EUMAEUS

All he wants is peace and quiet. He's had enough excitement—
(The door is thrown violently open. MELAS, *one of the more ardent suitors, thrusts* CLIA *aside, and enters. He's a powerful, handsome, dark-haired man of about thirty. He stands facing* PENELOPE.*)*

PENELOPE

Melas! How dare—

MELAS

So you let the pig-man visit you. But *we* have got to stay down in the hall.

PENELOPE

That was your promise! If you break it, you break my promise too. Get out of here, or I'll slash this work to pieces.
(She picks up the embroidery knife.)

MELAS

I came to tell you we're moving on. There isn't enough food left to feed the servants we had with us. We've sent them ahead of us to the harbour. The ship sails at noon.
(He looks over his shoulder at the open door, lowers his voice, and comes nearer to PENELOPE.*)*
I'll be back. I don't waste three years of my life.

PENELOPE

The others may have the same idea. They'll slip back here, one by one…

MELAS

I can deal with them singly.

PENELOPE

And are you so sure that they will come back singly, just to oblige you? Or even that *you'll* get back here, first?

CLIA

Let them leave, Penelope. Let them leave!
(She watches PENELOPE *anxiously, and a little puzzled with this talk.* PENELOPE *walks around the embroidery frame, looks at it, drops the knife, and begins to laugh.*
CLIA *exclaims)*

Penelope!

PENELOPE

(As MELAS *comes over to the frame to see what amuses her there)*

So you were going away, were you!

MELAS

It's almost finished! Why didn't you tell me?
(His voice is angry. PENELOPE *blocks the embroidery from his sight, as she looks up at him smilingly.)*

PENELOPE

But didn't I?

CLIA

Penelope! Are you insane?

MELAS

(Stares at her, and then begins to laugh)

You have your own brand of humour, haven't you?

ERYX

*(He speaks from the doorway, suddenly, and everyone
swings round in surprise to see he has been listening,
lounging against the doorpost, his hand on the knife
at his belt. ERYX is another of the suitors, about thirty-
five, red-haired, lean, crafty.)*

Which you were going to share with us, Melas? But of course
you were...

PENELOPE

(Moving to the centre of the room)

Leave, both of you! Before we have the whole mob up in my
room.

ERYX

(Soothingly)

I only came to keep an eye on him.

PENELOPE

And who is keeping an eye on you, Eryx?

ERYX

Now, now, Penelope. You don't seem to trust us.

(But he gives a quick look over his shoulder.)

Yet, here's one you *can* trust.

(He taps himself on the chest.)

See, I haven't put a foot inside your room, have I? And all I'd like to know is when that work of art will be finished. Today, tomorrow, or the next day?

PENELOPE
(Silencing CLIA *with a gesture)*
The next day.

ERYX
Hear that, Melas, old pal? Don't tell me that you distrust the lady's word. Come on, leave her in peace.
(His voice, when he is addressing MELAS, *is always hard, biting, sarcastic.)*

MELAS
(Moves away from the embroidery frame)
A couple of days should finish it.

ERYX
I'll take Penelope's word for it.
(To PENELOPE, *his voice now dripping politeness, and yet all the more menacing)*
At your service. Always. You'll remember that?
(He bows, and then leaves.)

PENELOPE
(To MELAS*)*
Now it's your turn to show me how noble at heart you really are.

MELAS

(Pointing to the embroidery frame)

Tell me, what's wrong with it?

PENELOPE

Aren't you leaving? Eryx will now be halfway toward the Hall.
He won't like it if—

MELAS

What's wrong?

(He still points.)

PENELOPE

Wrong?

MELAS

It's as rough as a five-day beard.

PENELOPE

Oh...that! Isn't it natural that I have been thinking of Ulysses,
and that I've wept? Tears don't help embroidery. But that's all
over now, all over.

(She smiles to EUMAEUS, *who looks nervously back,
while* CLIA *is horrified.)*

MELAS

You're worth waiting for. A woman who can weep for a man
long after he is dead is a wife worth having.

PENELOPE

I wish Ulysses could have heard that.

> *(She looks at* EUMAEUS *again.)*

EUMAEUS

It's just as well he didn't hear talk like that from a good-for-nothing drunk. And you listening to it!

PENELOPE

Ulysses jealous? Why, he never was. But then, I never gave him cause to be... Was that my mistake?

MELAS

> *(Who has advanced on* EUMAEUS, *meanwhile, and forced him to retreat behind the embroidery frame for safety)*

Who's a good-for-nothing drunk? Get back to your pigs, or you'll find yourself skewered over a fire with an apple stuck in your mouth.

> *(*MELAS *has drawn his sword, but* EUMAEUS *picks up the knife from the table and faces the advancing man.)*

EUMAEUS

> *(Suddenly dignified)*

I wasn't always a pig farmer. I've killed better men than you, in my day.

PENELOPE

> *(Moving swiftly between the men, as* MELAS *raises his sword to strike)*

There's to be no killing, here! Eumaeus, drop the knife and get back to your job.

(She pushes him toward the door as he drops the knife on the table, keeping herself between him and MELAS. As EUMAEUS leaves, MELAS takes a step after him, his sword still drawn.)

That would be foolish. For I'll never marry the man who kills anyone who belongs to this household. That's one man I'd *never* choose.

MELAS

(Hesitates, then sheathes his sword)

I'd do that for no one else except you.

PENELOPE

(Looking over her shoulder toward the doorway)

Isn't that silence very odd? What are they plotting? A surprise for you, Melas?

MELAS

(Moving quickly to the door)

Two more days, Penelope, and you'll choose a husband. Right?

PENELOPE

Two more days.

MELAS

You'll remember all I've done for you?

PENELOPE
I'll remember.
> (MELAS *smiles and leaves. She closes the door behind*
> *him, securely, and then begins to laugh quietly.)*

CLIA
> *(Her rage and dismay at last bursting free)*

Are you out of your mind? *What* have you done? *Penelope,*
what have you *done*?

PENELOPE
D'you know, I believe that ruffian thinks he *is* my protector.

CLIA
> *(Seizing* PENELOPE's *shoulders and shaking her as if she*
> *were a child)*

I'll tell you what you've done: you've kept these men here. You
could have let them ride off, but you—

PENELOPE
> *(Freeing herself angrily)*

Let them ride off and escape the punishment they've earned?
Let them sail away and invade some other island and keep its
people in misery?

CLIA
But—

PENELOPE
Stop fussing, Clia. I know what I'm doing.

(She hesitates, lowers her voice almost to a whisper.)
Ulysses has come home.

CLIA
(Terrified now)

My poor girl, my poor girl!... She's out of her mind... Penelope, can you hear me, can you understand me? Ulysses did not come back. Three men arrived by the fishing boats, this morning. But not one of them was Ulysses.

PENELOPE
(Startled)

Who gave you that news?

CLIA

Eumaeus. He told me. There's still no Ulysses. Penelope, what shall we do?

PENELOPE
(Smiling)

I'm going to rest. And to think. To think of a plan. Keeping those men here was only the first step... Now I must plan the next one, and the next...

CLIA

...She's waited too long...she's lost her reason.

PENELOPE
(She has walked over to her bedroom door, paying no attention to CLIA's hand-wringing. She pauses there, turns to say in a clear firm voice)

They'll leave, Clia. They'll all leave. But as *I* wish them to leave…
I'm the mistress of this house. And Ulysses is still its master.
(She goes out. The bedroom door closes quickly behind
her, and the curtain falls.)

SCENE 3

Later that morning.

PENELOPE *is sitting room is bathed in sunlight. Its door opens, a babel of mixed sounds follows* CLIA *and an elderly man into the room. He is white-haired, with a splendid head and good features. There is nobility and kindness in his face. He still wears his travelling boots and dusty cloak, and he carries a small harp.*

He is HOMER.

CLIA
(Calling excitedly as she enters and stands aside for
HOMER*)*

Penelope! Oh, she is still in her bedroom. Just a moment, and I'll fetch her.

(She has closed the door, after calling for PENELOPE, *and the room is quiet once more.)*

HOMER

Please don't disturb her. I'm quite content to wait here, if I may. That's a pretty rowdy crowd downstairs in the Hall. What are they celebrating?

CLIA

Victory.

HOMER

What victory?

CLIA

They think they've won. I don't know.
(She shrugs her shoulders helplessly.)
I just don't know anything any more. For three years, we've hoped they'd leave. This morning they were leaving. This noon,
(She looks at the bedroom door and shakes her head.)
they're staying.

HOMER

(Walking over to the window, looking round the room, examining everything)
I've never been in this room before. Charming. Cool, restful, quiet—just like Penelope herself.
(CLIA looks at him.)
I can remember hearing about Ulysses building this house: people didn't approve of his modern ideas in architecture—taking the beds out of the Hall and giving them private rooms! But I rather like this idea of separate sleeping quarters. Especially with the kind of guests you have.

CLIA

Guests? Invaders, that's what they are. Don't believe any of the stories they've been spreading around in the last three years. They can twist the truth quicker than a girl's smile.

HOMER
(Turning away from the window to look keenly at
CLIA*)*

Invaders. So that's the way it is. I must admit they weren't exactly what I had expected. You know, Clia, the sooner we get the news back to the mainland about the truth of this matter, the better for all of you.

CLIA
(Bitterly)

And haven't we tried? And who would listen? Last year, we even sent young Telemachus to the mainland to do some travelling—and to spread the truth. But would anyone believe him?

HOMER

Well...

CLIA

Yes, I know. The men sent rumours and lies ahead of the boy. He was jealous of them, they said. He had one of those mother...mother something-or-others.

HOMER

Mother fixations. Yes, I heard about that.

CLIA

And you heard about his wild imagination, too? And his pathetic exaggerations? Poor little fellow, trying to pretend he's a hero. Yes, they got everyone laughing at him, didn't they?

HOMER

People so often believe what it suits them to believe.
(He shakes his head sadly and moves to the centre of the room.)
At least I've brought you one piece of hope. Odysseus is alive. That is fact. Not rumour. And I've also learned that he is on his way home. He will soon be here.

CLIA

Soon? And what good will that do us *now*?
(She points to the embroidery frame.)
In two days, mark you—two days, that embroidery will be finished and Penelope will have to choose one of the men as a husband and—

HOMER

Embroidery? What's this about embroidery?
(He goes quickly over to the frame.)

CLIA

That's what it is, whatever it looks like. It's for the seventh and last chair. See—
(Points to the chairs along the wall)
six of them finished; and *that* makes seven.
(She points to the frame.)

HOMER
(Sharply)

What's this about seven chairs?

CLIA

It's the promise that Penelope gave. On the altar of Athena
herself. So that she could put off choosing a husband.

HOMER

Why, I always understood she promised to *weave* a shroud for
her father-in-law.

CLIA

Oh, at the last moment she changed her mind.

HOMER

But why wasn't I told about this change? I never heard about
any *embroidery*.

CLIA

Embroidery or weaving, it's all the same.

HOMER

On the contrary!... I have already composed a very fine poem
about Penelope weaving.

CLIA

So you *are* telling about Ulysses and Penelope? Isn't that nice!
Penelope!
(She knocks on the bedroom door, opens it a little.)

Penelope! You've a visitor; he's travelled a long way to see you!

PENELOPE
(Urgently)

Clia, don't tease me. Who is it?

CLIA
(To HOMER)

Poor dear! She's always thinking it might be Ulysses.
(To PENELOPE)

It's your friend the poet—the man who is making up the story about Ulysses.

(She leaves the bedroom door.)

HOMER

Clia, I don't make up stories... I describe the truth. That is why I am here in Ithaca now. If I didn't want to see the real facts for myself, I could stay in Smyrna, where I like the climate. And another thing—why do you call your master *Ulysses*? Give him his real name—Odysseus. Really, Clia... Ulysses! A complete bastardisation. It won't even scan properly.

CLIA

Penelope always calls him Ulysses. She says Odysseus is too big a mouthful. For instance,
(She points to ULYSSES' chair.)
you can say "Ulysses' chair" without too much of a splutter. But who's going to take a deep-enough breath to say "Odysseus's chair"?

HOMER
(Stiffly)

I still say Odysseus.

CLIA
(Placatingly)

Turned out a nice day, hasn't it? How far have you been travelling, this time?

HOMER

From Thessaly.

CLIA

Over all those mountains? My, that's quite a journey—
(She strikes her forehead.)
Your cloak—your boots—I was so excited I forgot to welcome you properly. I'll just rush downstairs and get a basin of water. I'm sorry, I really am...

HOMER
(Smiling again)

What I need most is a drink. I've walked from the village, and I've collected as much dust in my throat as on my boots.

CLIA

Shan't be a moment—
(As PENELOPE opens the bedroom door and enters the sitting room, CLIA exclaims and rushes out.)

PENELOPE

(Coming forward to HOMER *with hands outstretched.
She has changed her dress—she is now wearing a blue
silk gown, and her hair is charmingly arranged.)*
Homer! How wonderful to see you!… And how well you look.
(She takes his cloak and places it on one of the chairs.)

HOMER

You are looking remarkably well, yourself.
(He looks at her critically, though.)

PENELOPE

(Looking down at her dress)
You don't like it? I thought it was—quite—pretty.

HOMER

It's most charming, but isn't it a little—lighthearted? Not quite
what I had imagined you wearing.

PENELOPE

Really?
(She is amused. HOMER *has been looking for a place to
lay his harp. He almost puts it on* ULYSSES' *chair, but
then refrains.)*
Yes, put it there.

HOMER

But it's your husband's chair, and only Odysseus sits there.

PENELOPE

Put it on the chair. Ulysses will be honoured.

HOMER

My dear, I wish you'd call him Odysseus.

PENELOPE
(Laughing)

But my tongue trips over it.
(She pulls two chairs forward, and invites him to sit down.)
You always amaze me. You've never been in this room before,
yet you know all about Ulysses' chair.

HOMER

That's easily explained. People talk, you know. And poets listen.

PENELOPE

And when Homer sings, the people grow silent.

HOMER
(Now in very good humour)

If there's one thing nicer than being treated to a compliment,
it's having a pretty woman pay it.

PENELOPE

That wasn't a compliment; it was the truth. No poet is so—
*(She breaks off as the door opens. CLIA comes in with
a bronze basin of water and a folded towel over her
arm. AMARYLLIS follows her, carrying a large silver
goblet of wine.)*

What's this?

(She stares down at HOMER's *boots and springs to her feet.)*

Heavens! What have we done—or, rather, what haven't we done? Clia, you know the rule of this house: no stranger, however poor, arrives at our door without being welcomed. And what is our welcome?

CLIA

To speak kindly and invite him to enter; to bathe his hands and feet; to offer him bread and wine and a warm corner by the hearth.

HOMER

Now, now, Penelope... I always think of you as the gentlest woman I've ever met. Besides, you didn't notice my boots either, did you?

PENELOPE

No...

(She begins to laugh, too.)

All this excitement today is too much for me, I'm afraid.

(She draws aside CLIA, *who has placed the basin before* HOMER *and now kneels at his feet.)*

Let me.

(She kneels in front of HOMER *and begins to draw off his boots.* CLIA, *now on her feet, places the towel over* PENELOPE's *shoulder, and then beckons* AMARYLLIS *forward.* HOMER *takes the goblet quickly, has a long drink, and then raises it with a sigh of pleasure.)*

HOMER

Oh, come bring to me a pint of wine, and pour it in a silver tassie!

PENELOPE

Tassie? What on earth is that?

HOMER

A word I've just invented. Sounds amusing in a foreign kind of way, doesn't it? Not as heavy as "goblet," not as solemn as "beaker." Of course, you could get rid of that cold solemnity and add a touch of the sun by saying—now, let me see... Yes... "Come bring to me a pint of wine, a beaker full of the warm south." Full of the warm south... Yes, that stirs memories as well as one's palate.

(He nods, drinks, and sighs with pleasure as he slips his feet into the basin of water.)

AMARYLLIS

South is south, and north is north. You can't pour either of them into a beaker!

(She smiles saucily and tosses her head.)

HOMER
(Noticing her with amusement)
Ah, my public! How sensitive, how percipient, how appreciative! No wonder poets can starve to death.

CLIA
(Warningly)
Amaryllis! This isn't Melas you're talking to. It's Homer, the poet.

AMARYLLIS
(Unabashed)
He doesn't look as if he'll starve to death.

PENELOPE
Leave the room.

HOMER
(Laughing)
I'm going to take that as a compliment, Amaryllis.

AMARYLLIS
(All smiles, as she strikes a pretty pose for HOMER'S
benefit)
If it's a compliment you want, I can do better than that.

PENELOPE
(Flaring up)
If you don't leave this room at once, you'll leave this house.
*(*AMARYLLIS *looks at her angrily, and then goes out.)*

HOMER
Now, I'm afraid that was my fault somehow. My dear Penelope,
you're all on edge. This isn't like you.

PENELOPE
Isn't it?
(She bathes his feet for a moment, and then smiles.)
How much do you really know me, I wonder.

HOMER

You are one of the chief characters in my new poem. Of course
I know you. Well. How else could I make you come alive?

(PENELOPE *stares at him, and sits back on her heels,*
forgetting her duty.)

That was a pretty girl, all the same. Amaryllis, did you say? A
sweet name for a sweet face.

CLIA

And an empty head.

HOMER

Amaryllis... Amaryllis. There's music in the name. To play
with Amaryllis—to play with Amaryllis in the shade. No...to
sport with Amaryllis in the shade or with the tangles of Niobe's
hair...

(He shakes his head.)

That isn't quite right. Niobe—she's too tragic. I'll have to think
of someone else.

PENELOPE

(Smiling, fascinated by HOMER's *words, still sitting*
back on her heels)

To sport with Amaryllis...that sounds very appropriate to me.
I'd keep that phrase, at least. Are you thinking of using it in the
new poem? And the pint of wine, complete with tassie?—Oh,
Clia! We're listening to poetry being made!

HOMER

I'll use the phrases—if I can remember them. That's the trouble, you know: there are too many phrases running through my head. It's difficult to get them all into my poems.

PENELOPE

Then for every line of poetry you sing, there may be three that we shall never hear?

HOMER
(Cheerfully)

Sad, isn't it? That's why poets all go slightly crazy. Occupational disease. Now, what about this object?

(He lifts a foot to be dried, and brings PENELOPE back
to her duty again.)

Poor old feet! They've carried me many a mile. Why don't you rebel, feet? There isn't another part of my body that would take such a pounding and not complain...

(He speaks vaguely, as if listening and inventing.)

Oh—the moon shines bright on Mrs. Porter, and on her daughter, they wash their feet in soda water.

(He laughs.)

Don't think too much of that, do you, Penelope?

PENELOPE

Who's Mrs. Porter, and what's soda water? Or doesn't it matter when you're thinking up poetry?

(She laughs, too, as she finishes her task, and turns to
CLIA for a pair of sandals.)

But, Homer, quite seriously, it *is* such a waste not to use all the lines you invent—

*(*HOMER *is setting "Mrs. Porter" to a catchy little tune.)*
—even the silly ones.

HOMER

Waste? Why, I only plucked these words out of the air. If I don't use them, I send them back where they came from; and they'll hover around until another poet reaches up and catches them. There will always be plenty of poets. What I've lost, they'll find. So there's no waste.

(He bends to help PENELOPE *fasten on the sandals. He touches* PENELOPE'S *head.)*

Thank you. That was the sweetest welcome ever given me.

*(*CLIA *has removed the basin and towel and dusty boots, and bustles from the room. He helps* PENELOPE *to rise.)*

PENELOPE

Why don't you tell your phrases to your pupils? They could always use them.

HOMER

I teach my pupils *how* to sing, but I'll never teach them *what* to sing. There's such a thing as integrity, you know, even in the literary world. Besides, some of my pupils are getting too big for their tunics. Why, some day, they will be claiming that they helped to compose *The Iliad*.

PENELOPE

I loved *The Iliad*. I can hardly wait until your next poem comes out.

HOMER

(Sharply)

And *when* did you hear *The Iliad*?

PENELOPE

Oh, we've had several wandering minstrels during the last few years. They stay overnight, and sing to us, and it's always something from *The Iliad*. They say it's top of the request list, wherever they go.

HOMER

Were they from my School in Smyrna?

PENELOPE

Some were pupils of your pupils, I think.

HOMER

(Rising abruptly)

You see!—They'll be changing my lines, adding verses of their own! A hundred years from now, and I won't recognise some of my own poetry.

PENELOPE

A *hundred* years from *now*?

HOMER

What do you think I'm writing for? Only for the people who live today? Why, there's no reason for a good story to die. It can be passed down from mouth to mouth, from heart to heart, for at least a hundred years. Perhaps ten hundred.

PENELOPE

A thousand years? Oh, Homer, don't! The gods will hear you and be jealous.

HOMER
(Looking up humorously)
All right, gods. I take that back. No thousand years, but just whatever time it pleases you.
(To PENELOPE)
Is that better?

PENELOPE
(Shocked)
How can you talk that way? Aren't you afraid?

HOMER

I don't have to believe everything I sing about the gods, do I? If gods *are* godlike, then they are much too great to be flattered by the myths men create around them.

PENELOPE
(Teasingly)
I thought everything you composed was based on fact.

HOMER

I tell the truth about men and this man-world. But when it comes to gods—well, Penelope, you can be realistic about the earth, but all you can do is speculate about Heaven.

PENELOPE

What are you going to call your new poem?

HOMER

The Odyssey. The adventures of Odysseus on his long voyage home. When I arrived here this morning, I hoped to find Odysseus and get certain facts from him. I've heard plenty of rumours, of course—

PENELOPE
(Grimly)

So have I.

HOMER

But I have reliable information that he has left Calypso and her island, and is homeward bound. He's practically here, Penelope!

PENELOPE

If he doesn't meet another Calypso.

HOMER

Penelope, that isn't like you to be jealous—after all, Odysseus had—

PENELOPE

—trouble finding transportation. Yes, I've heard that one.

HOMER

Now, now, my dear—you've got to stop all this. You've got to start being Penelope again.

PENELOPE
(Pathetically)

But I *am* being Penelope.

HOMER

I remember Penelope as the patient, faithful wife, who waits for her husband to return from the war. She understands, and to understand is to forgive.

PENELOPE

Is it?

HOMER
(Ignoring that)

She is gentle, sweet, trusting, and kind. That's the Penelope I know. She's the sort of woman every man wants to come home to.

PENELOPE

And he'll get so bored with her that he'll run away again! Ulysses has had the taste of adventure, and of a woman like that—like that Calypso. Why, he spent *months* with her on that island!

HOMER

You are judging him before he can tell you what really happened. He may have been shipwrecked. He may have had to build another ship. He may have been ill. And it may have been the island's fault. It is perhaps a magic island—an island filled with noises, sounds, and sweet airs that give delight—and hurt not.

(He pauses for a second.)

Why! That's not bad, not bad at all. I'll try to remember that one. It isn't in my meter, though. Pity... Ah well... Penelope, haven't you ever dreamed of such an island? Most of us want a magic island, just now and again.

PENELOPE

(Bursting into tears, and throwing herself on his breast)

Oh, Homer, I'm so miserable!

(He tries to comfort her, clasping her awkwardly.)

You don't know what it's like to wait and wait and wonder if your husband will ever come back to you. Or, when he does, if he still loves you.

HOMER

He loves you. He's coming home, isn't he?

PENELOPE

(Drawing away, and in control of herself again)

Is he coming home because he loves me? Or is he tired of seeing the world and wouldn't it be nice to relax with quiet, sweet, gentle, kind Penelope for a while? That's not good enough!

HOMER

Penelope!

PENELOPE

You don't believe me? Oh, Homer, how blind you are!

(She begins to laugh.)

HOMER
(Sharply)

This is no laughing matter. Do you know what you're doing? You're ruining *The Odyssey.*

(He strides angrily to the frame.)

Yes, I've composed one of the best passages I've ever done—about you, sitting here, day by day, weaving at your loom. And you took up embroidery, instead. Oh, I should never have made a poem about a woman.

PENELOPE
(Subdued)

I didn't mean to ruin anything.

HOMER

You know I pride myself on the accuracy of my details—whether it's the wine-red sea at sunset; the mountain lion crouching on a jagged crag; or Helen, on the ramparts of Troy, walking in beauty like the night… And *you* had to go and embroider!

PENELOPE
(Helpfully)

But you could change—

HOMER

Change what I have composed? Not one word, not one image!

PENELOPE

Well—if anyone ever says you've been inaccurate about me, just blame it on your pupils who don't copy you correctly.

(Pause)

Homer, where's your sense of humour? Lost it? And I always loved it most of all.

> (HOMER, *who has been frowning at the ground, looks up—startled, as* PENELOPE'*s voice changes to unhappiness and entreaty.)*

Oh, I'm so *tired* of doing what everyone expects me to do... You've made *me* a prisoner, all of you. You've all got your fixed ideas of what I ought to be. Clia believes that Ulysses' wife must be brave and eternally hopeful. Telemachus thinks it is quite natural that I should live a dull, dreary life—mothers aren't supposed to be young or human! Even Amaryllis takes it for granted that I'm too old to envy the laughter and singing that I can hear from the Hall, night after night. "Noble Penelope," you all say, "sweet Penelope. Of course we can depend on you." Flattering? Yes. And there's no snare so insidious as that of flattery. Little by little, I've become a prisoner of my own vanity, with all of you looking at me admiringly as you tighten the knots around me. But I want to be free. I want to be Penelope again, before she is completely trapped.

(Silence complete)

HOMER
(Coming to PENELOPE, *putting his arm around her shoulder)*

My dear Penelope.

PENELOPE
(Dejectedly)

Now I *have* ruined *The Odyssey.*

HOMER
(Gently)

No... No... You've altered nothing, nothing that is essential.

PENELOPE

But I've so little patience; and I'm frightened and heartsick. And I'm so bad at weaving—that's really why I changed to embroidery.

HOMER

Trivia, trivia—all of them. The main thing is: you love Odysseus.

PENELOPE

Yes, but I can't help that.

HOMER

And you've been loyal to him.

PENELOPE

Because I'm in love with him. That isn't being noble...that's just being logical.

HOMER
(Smiling)

Is it?... Then it's such strong logic that all those little things you worry about don't really matter very much. They are only bitterness that comes from lonely nights. The moment you see Odysseus—you'll forget all that. And what then remains? The simple truths of loyalty and love—the essentials that make you what you really are.

PENELOPE

I still feel I've got into your poem under false pretences.

HOMER

Do you think I judge a man or a woman by the little things? There's more to a human being than words and arguments, laughter and tears. A man with high courage can know fear. A man who loves may know bitterness. A man who keeps faith can have moments of doubts. Do we add up the fears, the bitterness, the doubts, and make them our answer? Or do we see the courage, the faith, the love that has kept him—in spite of every attack—from being a coward and traitor? Penelope, Penelope...what do you admire in a tree? Only the pretty leaves? Leaves wither and fall. Or do you praise the branches and admire their strength? They too can fall. But what about the roots? If they are good, the tree will ride out every storm, and bloom each new spring.

PENELOPE
(Shaking her head)
You make me seem better than I am. You ought to have chosen a heroine who wouldn't have disappointed you.

HOMER

Where would I have found her? I wanted a symbol of loyalty and love. I chose you.
(He begins to pick up his cloak, his harp.)
Your story is what I needed. I needed? It is what we all need.
(He touches her shoulder, and leaves abruptly.)

PENELOPE

*(Walking slowly downstage, and wiping away a little
tear)*

So, I'm a symbol.

(She half smiles.)

Why couldn't he have left me just a woman? But no—I'm a
symbol... Well, what is a symbol supposed to do now?

(Suddenly angry)

Welcome her wandering husband with a smile? A *symbolic* smile?

(As suddenly miserable)

Athena! Help me... In the name of Reason, what should I do?

(The goddess ATHENA *comes through the wall and
stands watching* PENELOPE. *She remains invisible to all
the mortals in this story, but when she addresses them,
her voice speaks in their minds. And so now,* PENELOPE
is not aware of ATHENA, *and her answers to* ATHENA *are
spoken as a monologue rather than as replies to* ATHENA's
interruptions. ATHENA, *in flowing white, is calm and
cool. She speaks with wry humour in her voice.)*

ATHENA

It's about time you called me.

PENELOPE

I need advice.

ATHENA

Delighted as always... But if I give it, will you take it?

PENELOPE

Hear me, Athena! I've prayed to you all these years...

ATHENA

I've brought your husband back to Ithaca, haven't I?

PENELOPE

And now Ulysses is here; and Homer expects me to be the sweet, understanding wife. No tears. No questions. That's hard to do... Is it even fair?

ATHENA

Let's just call it reasonable.

PENELOPE

It *isn't* reasonable. It's the last straw. That's all.

ATHENA

Hold on there! Who's the expert on Reason, anyway? You or I?

PENELOPE

Or is it reasonable?... After all, I *want* Ulysses. Tears and reproaches might drive him away.

ATHENA

He never found them fascinating.

PENELOPE

But boredom could also drive him away.

ATHENA

He doesn't plan to be bored, my sweet.

PENELOPE

Why—Homer's picture of Penelope bored even me!

ATHENA

Look, you're arguing in circles. Do you love Ulysses or don't you?

PENELOPE

Ulysses is all my life. If he has come home only from a sense of duty, of decency, of pity—I think I'd die.

ATHENA

Will you stop being so emotional? Or you'll drive *me* away. As you did this morning when you enticed those men to stay.

PENELOPE

Oh...

ATHENA

And don't blame me. Reason had nothing to do with you this morning. Impulse, instinct, that's what it was. Why *did* you do it? To punish Ulysses? For what?

PENELOPE

Taking all these years to travel home... Calypso and her silly island... And when he does get here, he slinks ashore and hides. Why? Doesn't he trust me?... That hurts. That hurts deeply. And yet—

ATHENA

(Turning to the audience)

This is known as woman's logic. Interesting, isn't it?

PENELOPE

—and yet—I don't want to hurt him. All I want him to prove is that he is willing to fight for me, because he loves me.

ATHENA

And you never thought of punishing him, just a little? You never thought of making him jealous? Now, Penelope, be quite frank with yourself!

PENELOPE

(Stamping her foot)

Did he expect to walk into our Hall, and I was to say, "Ulysses, darling! You're late for dinner; shall I scramble you some eggs"?

ATHENA

So instead, you prepared eleven swords to point at his throat.

PENELOPE

No, no, no... I have other ideas. He won't even have to fight those men! I'll arrange a contest, a contest that Ulysses is bound to win. I want him to remember this home-coming forever. I want this day to be the climax of all his adventures.

ATHENA

He was always a man for a climax. Good, Penelope. Very good. Now I'm with you. Jealousy is a mean, emotional business that I leave to Venus when she's spited. But to teach a man the reality of true values—yes, there I'm with you. Teaching is my favourite profession, even if it's underpaid.

PENELOPE

Ulysses will stay here...never leave me again...

ATHENA

Certainly, he'd never risk another home-coming like this one. Only, be sure you plan your contest well. Plan *very* well. And I'll do my part: I'll get him here, today.

PENELOPE
(Sighing)

Homer would never approve of all this. But I did try to tell him I wasn't really a heroine. I'm just a woman who's married to a hero, that's all. It frightens me, when I think of it. The greatest hero of the whole Trojan War, and he's married to Penelope!... Now stop this, Penelope, stop it! He's coming home, isn't he? So keep him.
(She moves quickly upstage toward the bedroom.)
What dress shall I wear? Shall I braid my hair, or leave it loose?
(Her voice fades as she enters the bedroom, leaving the door slightly ajar.)

ATHENA

Call me when you make up your mind.
(To the audience)
I do get so tired hovering around while you human beings decide—will you, won't you, will you, perhaps, maybe. I feel

like an equation, waiting to be solved.

> *(She is walking round the room as she speaks, and*
> *now she stops to look at the embroidery on the frame.)*

Hm! You probably can't see this from where you're sitting, but I think that's just as well. Frankly, it's terrible!

> *(She shudders and comes well downstage.)*

Poor Penelope, she really *has* suffered—whoever told her she could embroider? It certainly wasn't the Goddess of Reason.

> *(PENELOPE is heard singing "Mrs. Porter." ATHENA, hand*
> *on hip, taps her foot.)*

She's got five dresses out now, wondering which to choose. As if Ulysses will look at the dress! Why don't we give her ten minutes to change her mind several times? Then we can get on with Act Two.

> *(ATHENA, now downstage centre, looks around the audience.)*

Ten minutes?

> *(She smiles and nods agreement. She gestures to the*
> *wings, and the curtains close obediently.)*

ACT II

We are in the Great Hall of Ulysses' house. Here, the daily life of eating, cooking, talking, sitting goes on.

So, downstage left, we have the hearth and open fireplace; some pots; a basin; two leather-seated stools. Downstage right, there is the dining area: a long table, placed parallel with the right-hand wall; long wooden side benches; and the master's chair at the head of the table. Upstage, on the left, we have a few shallow stairs, leading to a dais from which the door into the women's quarters (and PENELOPE'S private apartment) opens. Upstage right, a similar narrow door to the men's quarters. In the centre of the back wall, there is the main entrance to the Hall. Its large double doors are open to ventilate the Hall and light it by day, with the help of some narrow windows high up on the side walls. Storage chests lie against the wall under the windows. (A man standing on one of them could see out, but an outsider couldn't see into the Hall.) On the walls, too, are *four large brackets for holding torches: one near the fireplace; one on the back wall, near the dais; one, balancing it, on the back wall to the right; one near the dining table. And to the right of the main entrance we see a few small shields decorating the wall, while to the left of the door is the Great Bow. It hangs in solitary splendour, between the corner dais and the entrance. As it is unstrung, it doesn't look much of a weapon—just two long ibex horns, fastened together at their roots by a strong handgrip of bronze and leather, their points recurved outward, with its string attached at one end and hanging free. The passage of time in the first two scenes is marked by the gradual shift of sun that pours over the threshold, moving toward the dais.*

SCENE 1

Full sunlight is now streaming into the Hall. The dining table is in disorder from the midday meal. We can hear that some of the suitors have already reached the courtyard; three others are leaving the Hall slowly, teasing AMARYLLIS *(who doesn't object) as she starts to help* CLIA *with the bowls and cups on the table.* MELAS *still sits in the chair at the head of the table, finishing his wine slowly. Over by the hearth,* HOMER *stands silent, watchful. The babel of voices from the courtyard diminishes gradually.*

CLIA
(Bundling bowls into AMARYLLIS'S *apron, and then bustling to the hearth to attend the fire)*
Take them out to the stream. Scour them well. Use plenty of sand. I don't want any stains left on them, this time.

AMARYLLIS

You've given me too many. Don't blame me if they get dented. And stop scolding me. All day it has been nothing but nag nag nag.

(*She rearranges the thin copper bowls in her apron as she talks, dumping some out on the table in protest; and then, as she catches a glare from* CLIA, *puts them back. She speaks to* MELAS.*)*

Enjoyed your dinner?

(MELAS *pays no attention. She moves nearer.*)

It's my night off.

(MELAS, *without looking at her, waves her away.*)

All right, Mr. Sourface, I can get one of the others to take me into the village.

MELAS

(*Still not looking at her*)

Will you stop pestering me?

AMARYLLIS

I like that! What's come over you—

MELAS

Shut your mouth! Can't a man get some peace around here?

(*He avoids her eyes and pours some more wine into his goblet. He stretches himself comfortably.*)

AMARYLLIS

Look at you! Sitting in the master's chair. So you think Penelope is going to choose *you*!

(*She laughs.*)

MELAS

Clear out!

(*He throws his wine in her face.*)

You talk too much.

AMARYLLIS

(*In sudden rage*)

Too much? I haven't talked enough. Penelope has been laughing at you, all along.

CLIA

(*From the hearth where she is sweeping*)

Amaryllis!

AMARYLLIS

Why, you fool, she could have finished that embroidery months and months ago.

(MELAS *looks at her now.*)

She's been ripping it out, every night. And only a man wouldn't have noticed!

(MELAS *rises, staring.* CLIA *rushes at* AMARYLLIS, *the hearth broom upraised, but the girl runs out into the yard.*)

MELAS

(*Catching* CLIA's *arm*)

So it's true, is it?

(*He twists her arm as she struggles.*)

HOMER
(Coming quickly forward)
Stop that! Respect for age is the first virtue.

MELAS
(Aiming a last blow at CLIA's *head as he lets her go)*
I've been tricked, is that it? Tricked...

CLIA
(Retreating behind HOMER*)*
See how they behave! At dinner, they pretended to be so reasonable, just to impress you. But now you see a touch of what they really are.

ERYX
(Enters from the yard. He carries a spear in his hand.)
Come on, you! We're going hunting. We'll find a deer, up the Green Mountain. We're tired of eating stewed slop.

MELAS
I'm staying here.
(He walks back to the table, sits down.)

ERYX
You're coming with us. You don't stay here alone. Get that?

MELAS
A trick—
(He crashes his fist on the table.)

ERYX

(Injured innocence)

A trick? I'm playing no trick—we're just going out hunting on the Green Mountain. That's all.

MELAS

Nothing but a god-damned trick.

(He reaches for the wine.)

ERYX

You're drunk. What do you think you're celebrating anyway? Get out of that chair!

MELAS

Leave me alone.

(He drinks and waves ERYX aside.)

I've some thinking to do.

ERYX

You?

(He laughs, but then falls silent as MELAS rises suddenly and stares at the door which leads to PENELOPE's room.
ERYX looks at CLIA, who is obviously afraid.)

What's been going on?

CLIA

Nothing...it's nothing. Just a silly story that Amaryllis invented. And he believed her!

(She tries to sound amused.)

ERYX

Just a silly story, eh? And aren't you going to share it with the rest of us, Melas? Or do I have to hear it from Amaryllis herself?

MELAS

Then get set for a shock. Penelope has been ripping out that embroidery, night after night.

ERYX

WHAT?

MELAS
(His voice rising)
She never meant to finish it. She's turned weeks into months, months into years. We've been swindled, all of us.

CLIA
(Quickly)
I tell you, Amaryllis is crazy with jealousy, she's—

ERYX

Sure, sure. Jealousy is a liar. But it can also tell a sharp truth when it chooses.
(He takes a step forward, threateningly.)

MELAS

Don't waste your time on her. She'd swear blue is yellow to protect Penelope. But she gave away the truth when she rushed at Amaryllis.

HOMER

That isn't any proof at all. It would never stand up in court.

MELAS

I've got enough proof. I saw the embroidery today. Now I know why it was such a god-damned mess.

(To CLIA*)*

Get your mistress down here!

*(*CLIA *doesn't move.)*

All right, I'll fetch her myself. I'll teach her a new trick or two.

(He springs toward the steps, but ERYX *is even quicker. He catches* MELAS *roughly by the arm and swings him around.* MELAS *whips out his short sword.* ERYX *raises his spear watchfully.)*

ERYX

(Extremely dangerous, now, although his voice is quiet enough)

We're all in this. Don't forget that!

HOMER

(Watching them face each other, about to fight)

That could always be one solution. Go ahead, gentlemen!

(To ERYX*)*

But drop that spear and use your sword. Equal weapons, you know.

ERYX

(To MELAS*)*

The old boy made a point there. Why fight? Not much future in that for either of us.

MELAS

Sure—especially when I'm the best swordsman around here. Go on! Equal weapons—if you dare!

(A man's shadow falls over the threshold. A beggar stands there, hesitant. It is ULYSSES, *dressed in his tattered wool cape, his traveller's hat pulled well down over his forehead, his shoulders drooping, his whole appearance that of age and weakness. No one pays the slightest attention to him, as he stands humbly by the left side of the door.)*

ERYX

Use your brains! If you are crazy enough to pick a fight, what then? Either you kill me, or I kill you—

HOMER

What's wrong with that?

ERYX

—but there are nine other men left. Is the winner going to fight them all, too? Will they wait to be picked off, one by one?

MELAS
(Lowers his sword)

All right, then. But I'm going to wait no longer. Let Penelope choose now.

(He walks back to the head of the table.)

ERYX

Choose? Just how will she choose?

MELAS

(Shrugging his shoulders, one hand on the master's chair)

I'll agree to stick by her decision.

ERYX

Isn't that generous of you? You think you're her favourite!

(He faces MELAS angrily, again, his spear ready.)

MELAS

(Ready with his sword, but confident and smiling)

It's all a gamble, anyway. I told you that when we first came here.

ERYX

Then why don't we throw dice and let them choose the winner?

MELAS

(Angry, now, and shouting)

Because none of us would have a fair chance if you got your hands on a set of dice.

HOMER

Gentlemen, gentlemen! Really, this could go on forever.

CLIA

It has been going on for three years.

HOMER

Frankly, I don't think you'll ever find a solution, for each wants to win and no one intends to be the loser. When you came here, no doubt you thought there was strength in numbers; but now, your numbers defeat you. Oh, happy band of brothers!

ERYX

You keep out of this!

HOMER

I wish I could. Oh, why didn't you leave this morning, before I ever arrived!

ERYX
(Very softly)

You know, I almost forgot that... *Penelope kept us here.* I wonder why?...
(He and MELAS *lower their weapons.* ULYSSES *straightens his back for a moment, and then bows his head to stare at the ground once more.)*
I don't like this. Come on. We'll both see Madame Penelope. Now.
(He and MELAS *move purposely together toward the steps.)*

HOMER

You did mention nine others, who seem to have a part-interest in this too. Shouldn't you at least appear to consult them? Clia, will you step into the yard and inform—

ERYX

(Speaking to CLIA *as* MELAS *turns on* HOMER*)*

You'll find them at the stables. Tell them that Penelope's little comedy is over. Bring them here. We'll make her choice for her.

PENELOPE

(Suddenly appearing from her doorway. She pauses at the top of the steps, watching HOMER *standing his ground as* MELAS *and* ERYX *advance on him.* PENELOPE *is carefully dressed in green, in a chiffon robe of flowing grace. There are jewels in her high-coiled hair. She has never looked more beautiful. But for one moment, too, she looks a little frightened. Then the goddess* ATHENA *emerges from the wall and stands on the dais near* PENELOPE. PENELOPE *recovers herself.)*

Will you, indeed? That was not the bargain we made.

ERYX

(Swinging round, along with MELAS, *to see* PENELOPE *on the dais)*

You broke the bargain.

PENELOPE

I? I broke my word?

MELAS

You ripped out that embroidery as fast as you stitched it.

PENELOPE

But—but—I *never* made any promise *not* to rip it out.

ATHENA
(Relaxes and smiles)
Not bad, not bad at all. But be careful, Penelope, careful!
*(HOMER is laughing now; and ERYX and MELAS look at
each other.)*

PENELOPE
And haven't you broken your promise to keep out of this Hall
for two hours each afternoon, so that I can walk in peace?
(ERYX and MELAS exchange a second stare.)

ERYX
Look here—who's questioning whom?

PENELOPE
Please don't shout. After all, there is only one more day before
I make my choice, so why annoy me?... You see, I admit
you've won.

HOMER
(Shocked)
Penelope!

MELAS
(Going toward her)
In that case, why not choose now?
(His voice is gentle; his smile is charming.)

PENELOPE

A personal choice would be—invidious. Certainly difficult. Perhaps even a little dangerous. I've a better idea: I choose a *contest* in which you will all have an equal chance. That's fair, isn't it?

ERYX
(Delighted)

We'll choose the contest.

PENELOPE
(Sweetly)

But can you? Can you agree on the choice of weapons?
(She watches ERYX *and* MELAS *exchange looks.)*
Then that's settled—I'll announce the contest tomorrow night.

ERYX

You'll do it *now.*

MELAS

Yes, *now.*

ATHENA

I *told* you to be careful... Oh, why don't you look at the doorway?

PENELOPE
(Coming down the steps)

But I—I first must go to Athena's altar, and offer her some flowers, and a prayer... You know how cross she can get, if things aren't done properly.

ATHENA

Well, really!

ERYX

No more delays, Penelope. It's now. Or never.
(He and MELAS *take a quick step to intercept* PENELOPE *as she hurries toward the door. She now can see the beggar, and halts suddenly.* ATHENA *folds her arms and leans against a wall. No one, of course, is aware of her physically. She stands there, seeing but unseen.)*

PENELOPE

Who—who's this?

ERYX
(Sarcastically)

A beggar, I believe.

ULYSSES
(Takes a step forward humbly, touching his hat)
Asking your help, lady. Some food, a place to sleep.

PENELOPE
(In a low voice)

Oh, Clia!

CLIA
(Apologetically)

I haven't had time to welcome him properly. At first, I didn't see him, and then when I did, you came into the Hall, and—

ERYX

That's right! Change the subject.

MELAS

Oh no, she doesn't!
                    (Roughly, to PENELOPE)
Announce the contest.

PENELOPE
                    (Turning away from the door)
Now?

HOMER

No! Penelope, don't! Don't give in!

PENELOPE
            (Ignoring HOMER, and smiling to MELAS and ERYX)
What about the others? Shouldn't they be here, too?

ERYX

We've had enough delay. You tell us; we'll tell them.

PENELOPE
            (Pausing at the foot of the steps)
I said the contest would be fair to all. None of you has ever shot
with a great bow, has he?

MELAS

One of those old things our grandfathers used to shoot with?
Why, there hasn't been one of them around in years.

PENELOPE
(Pointing to the unstrung bow that rests on the wall
beside the door)

There is one... I'll marry the man who can string that bow and shoot an arrow through a hole bored in the head of an axe. We'll drive the handle of the axe into the earth floor, over there, at the far end of this Hall.

(Now, she points to the back of the auditorium, and
everyone on stage turns to look.)

You are all good marksmen. You will all have the same chance. What could be fairer?

ERYX
(Looks at the Great Bow)

So that's a great bow, is it? I always thought it was some old yoke for a pair of decrepit oxen.

HOMER
(Angrily)

It's a noble contest—heroic, in fact. Too good for any of you.

(Sadly, to PENELOPE*)*

So you no longer think of yourself as the wife of Odysseus? You feel free to marry one of them?

(He gestures with distaste to MELAS *and* ERYX.*)*

PENELOPE

I'll marry the man who wins the contest. It will be open to *everyone who is in this Hall* tonight. Except Telemachus, of course—there's no Oedipus complex in *our* family.

ERYX

See what you could win, Homer?
(*He and* MELAS *enjoy this joke, but* HOMER *turns away from* PENELOPE.)

HOMER

I want no part of this.
(*At his bitterness,* PENELOPE's *head droops. She covers her eyes, and runs toward the door on the dais.* ATHENA *shrugs her shoulders once more, and walks slowly back into the wall.*)

ERYX

(*As he sees* MELAS *edging over toward the bow*)
Hands off!

MELAS

I was only looking.

ERYX

We'll keep it that way. We'll go up the Green Mountain and kill some meat. We'll have a banquet tonight.

MELAS

You're accepting the contest?

ERYX

We can talk it over with the others. Perhaps we'll think of a better one, and use that old bow for kindling.

HOMER

Barbarians! Respecters of nothing except your own will-to-power! The history of that bow is—

MELAS

Save your breath and compose a wedding song for Penelope.

ERYX

(To CLIA*)*

Tell her we'll be back, before the shadow reaches there!
(As he speaks, he gashes a line with a sudden stroke of his spear on the sun-covered threshold. Then he elbows the beggar aside, and MELAS *follows him with another shove at the beggar. They hurry out, grimly amused.)*

CLIA

(Covering her eyes)

Oh, Penelope!

HOMER

(Goes over to the beggar)

Come in, come in. Don't judge us by the company we are forced to keep.

CLIA

(Remembering her duties)

Yes, come in, you're welcome, you really are.
(To HOMER*)*
Oh, what are we going to do?
(To the beggar)

Just go over there by the fire. Yes, there.

(To HOMER)

I must go to Penelope. You hurt her. Did you see the way you hurt her?

(To the beggar)

Sit down, sit down. I shan't be a minute. I haven't forgotten my manners; it's just that we've a lot of trouble in this house.

(She hurries to the dais. From outside, there is a clatter of horses' hoofs in the distance, diminishing)

HOMER

I didn't think my words would hurt Penelope, not this new and different Penelope.

CLIA

(Opening the door to the women's quarters and halting there for a moment)

Then perhaps she isn't so different, after all.

HOMER

A woman without faith is a woman without virtue; and a man without loyalty is a man without honour. But tell her—tell her I'm sorry. I did not mean to hurt her in front of everyone.

CLIA

You didn't?

(She gives a disbelieving laugh, and goes out.)

HOMER

(Staring at the closed door)

Perhaps I did...

(He turns and walks thoughtfully over to the hearth.
The beggar is now seated by the fireplace.)

We gave you a poor welcome, I'm afraid. And the advice I'm going to give you now will sound still poorer. Don't stay! Leave!

ULYSSÉS

But I've just got here.

HOMER

Don't you understand the situation? This house is occupied territory. Its invaders were too divided to win any complete victory, but—

ULYSSES

Then why worry?

HOMER

Because we are now giving in. We are helping them to win. Don't you see? They had the power of numbers, and ruthlessness to match. We only had a moral strength.

(ULYSSES yawns.)

Ah, I see I am holding your complete interest.

(He looks with distaste at the beggar.)

Let me put it another way—I'm serious about this; stop yawning and listen! As our strength weakens, their power grows. They will come back from the Green Mountain drunk with the sense of victory. So leave now, while you can.

ULYSSES

What's your stake in this?

HOMER

Why, I'm just a visitor, like you.

ULYSSES

Why don't you leave, then?

HOMER

I've been wondering about that. Perhaps I've praised courage so often in my songs, that I've sung myself into staying.
(He rubs his head ruefully, ULYSSES only settles himself more comfortably on the bench.)
You don't believe my warning?

ULYSSES

I'll leave when you leave.

HOMER

Have it your own way. But if you *are* staying, why not be comfortable? Take off your cloak and hat.

ULYSSES

(Pulling his cloak over his legs)
First, I'll warm my bones at the fire. Draughty places, these big halls.

HOMER

(Taking a seat opposite ULYSSES, on the other side of the hearth with its low but steady fire)
You've travelled far?

ULYSSES

Far enough.

HOMER

That's quite a journey. Where are you going?

ULYSSES

Home.

HOMER

Talkative fellow, aren't you?

ULYSSES

Tired men prefer sleep.

HOMER

But you must wash and eat, first. Then you can sleep all afternoon, until those barbarians return. There won't be much sleep for anyone then. Do you mind if I ask you a question or two? I was hoping you could give me some news.

ULYSSES

When I travel, I mind my own business. Then I don't run into trouble.

HOMER

I see. You prefer to walk into it, as you did today.
(There's a moment of complete silence. Then HOMER
tries again.)
On your travels, did you hear anything of Odysseus?

ULYSSES

Odysseus? Who's that?

HOMER

You are sitting in his house.

ULYSSES

I am? Odysseus...

HOMER

He was the greatest general we had against the Trojans. He won the war for us.

ULYSSES

Wasn't that the fellow who got killed?

HOMER

He's alive. He's travelling home, just like you.

ULYSSES

Well, I hope he had a better journey than I had. You a friend of his?

HOMER

I'd be honoured if he would call me that. Actually, I never met him. He was off on a secret mission when I visited the Trojan front. I was so sure that he'd be home by this time that I made a special journey to visit his house.

ULYSSES

Why?

HOMER

You'd rather ask questions than answer them, I think. You don't know who I am, do you?

ULYSSES

Can't say I do.

HOMER

I am Homer.

ULYSSES

Glad to meet you. Noman is the name.
                (He taps himself on the chest.)
What's your line of business? Or are you retired?

HOMER

I hope not. I'm a poet. A man who makes verses. I've been telling about the heroes of the Trojan War.

ULYSSES

Must be quite a story.

HOMER

But you can take it or leave it, eh?

ULYSSES

Well, heroes are just people.

HOMER
(Sharply)
Have you ever met a hero?

ULYSSES
Who knows a hero when he meets one?

HOMER
You certainly wouldn't. What's your trade?

ULYSSES
A bit of everything, and nothing very much. A hunter, mostly.

HOMER
Boars?
(He's interested, now.)

ULYSSES
I've met them too on my travels.

HOMER
(Angry again)
I meant wild boars. Have you ever hunted them?

ULYSSES
Sure, sure…

HOMER
Splendid! You see, I'm composing a description of a boar hunt for my new book, and this particular hunt is the famous one

when Odysseus was gashed in the leg by a boar's tusk.

ULYSSES

Working the boar pretty close, wasn't he?

HOMER

(Severely)

He killed it. But, what I must find out is this: when a boar attacks, how does he—

ULYSSES

Odysseus... That's the fellow who owns this house?

HOMER

(Rising in disgust)

The delayed-reaction type, I see.

ULYSSES

Him?

HOMER

(Turning away)

No. Not *him,* as you say so eloquently.

ULYSSES

Nice place he's got here, anyway.

(He grins, watching HOMER'S *retreat.)*

Pretty nice, *pretty* nice, if you ask me.

(He stretches his legs and relaxes.)

Not bad at all.

HOMER

That's what some other men think, too.

*(*ULYSSES*'s smile fades,* CLIA *enters, and hurries down from the dais.* HOMER *forgets the beggar.)*

How is Penelope? Did you tell her I was sorry? Of course, I still disagree with what she's done, but I should never have—

CLIA

I told her. But she just sat there, clasping her hands.

HOMER

(Somewhat taken aback)

Oh...

CLIA

Twice, she said: "Was I right? Or did I guess wrong?" And I said, "Now whether you were right or wrong, honey, we'll just have to wait until those men get back here tonight. *Then* we'll know."—Heaven help us!

HOMER

Her conscience has begun to trouble her.

CLIA

Then she said, "*Could* I have been mistaken?"

HOMER

You see!

CLIA

But she answered herself, this time. "No," she said, "no. I *was* right. I could feel it. In here." And she clasped her hands over her heart.

HOMER

Clia!—Is Penelope ill? She has been living under too great a strain—

CLIA

But wait until you hear the end! Up she jumps, throws her arms around me, and dances around the room. She was singing that song she's picked up from you. About Mrs. Porter and her daughter. I left *then*.

(She turns to ULYSSES.*)*

I'll get you freshened up in no time, before Penelope comes downstairs to welcome you.

(She goes over to fetch a basin from a wall.)

ULYSSES
(Startled)

Welcome *me*?

CLIA

So she said. And why not?

ULYSSES

But—I'm just a—beggar, someone of no account.

CLIA

(To HOMER, *as she bustles across to the door into the yard)*
He's a stranger to this part of the world, all right. Nora!
Icantha!... One of you girls—bring some water!
(She returns to the hearth, places the basin in front of
ULYSSES, *and lifts a kettle of hot water from the fire.)*

ULYSSES

Don't trouble, please don't—

CLIA

(Pouring some hot water into the basin)
I wish that was all the trouble we had to worry about. Wait,
now, wait! Let me help you with your boots.
(But ULYSSES *is too quick for her.)*
Independent character, aren't you?

HOMER

It's good to find a house where the old rules of hospitality are
still respected. People have got careless since the war. And
selfish, too. There's a general lowering of standards—it's all
most worrying.

CLIA

Why blame the war? Any excuse is a good excuse for some
people.
(Stopping ULYSSES, *as he is about to put a foot into*
the basin)
Take your time. It's much too hot. What's the hurry, anyway?
*(*AMARYLLIS *enters from the yard, carrying a vase of*

water on her shoulder. She looks nervously at CLIA, *and hesitates.* CLIA *glances over her shoulder.)*

Oh! It's you, Miss Troublemaker.

AMARYLLIS

I didn't mean to—

CLIA

You didn't mean it! That's another excuse we can do without. Well, stop standing there, posing like a dancing girl. Can't you see we're waiting?

> (AMARYLLIS *comes over to the hearth. She is partly afraid of* CLIA, *partly curious about the stranger.* CLIA *takes the vase of water, and pours some of it into the basin and tests it. She notices* AMARYLLIS' *interest in the beggar.)*

Yes, have a good look. But I don't think he's your style. What's wrong with your cheek? It's bruised. And you've been crying—

AMARYLLIS

And they twisted my arm, and they—

CLIA
(More gently)

So you've decided we are your friends, after all. Stop crying, and get me a towel. A *clean* towel.

AMARYLLIS

They were trying to make me tell all I know about Penelope. But I didn't say a thing.

153

CLIA

You had already said it. Where's the towel?

AMARYLLIS

They are all gathered together, and they are saying terrible things—if Penelope is tricking them, they'll—

HOMER
(Striding quickly to the door)
Let them talk. What I fear is action. Sudden, irrational action.
(He looks out into the yard, and then beyond.)
No, it's all right. They've taken the path to the Green Mountain. All of them.
(He sighs with relief, but he still watches the men in the distance.)
And stop gloating over our troubles, Amaryllis. I can imagine our possible future more fully than you could ever describe it.
(AMARYLLIS tosses her head, and moves over to one of the chests by the wall, where she searches for a towel. HOMER watches the path to the mountain. CLIA begins bathing the stranger's feet, talking to him as she does so.)

CLIA

If you've got to clutch that rag around you, hold it a bit higher, will you? You're safe with me. I've buried three husbands, and I'm not looking for any more, thank you. There, that's better.
(She pulls up the cloak over his knee. She stiffens, suddenly, with her hand on his leg.)
What's this?

*(She looks down, staring at the large scar which begins
just below his knee.)*

Why it's—

*(ULYSSES clamps one hand over her mouth and chokes
off the word. With his other hand, he grasps her
shoulder, and he leans forward to look intently into
her eyes. Then he lets her go, still watching her. CLIA
sits back on her heels, quite motionless, staring at him.
She begins, slowly, to bathe his feet as AMARYLLIS calls
over from one of the chests.)*

AMARYLLIS

I've looked and looked. This is the best I can find.

(She comes over to the hearth with a white towel.)

And don't blame me—it's Nora who does the laundry.

*(CLIA takes the towel in silence. AMARYLLIS looks
surprised. Then she sees that the stranger is watching
her, and she smiles at him as she moves to a corner of
the hearth where she can strike a pretty pose as she
looks down at him.)*

Where did you come from, stranger?

ULYSSES

Sparta.

AMARYLLIS

And what's your name?

CLIA

Finish your work, Amaryllis.

AMARYLLIS

I've cleaned all the dishes. They are drying, out in the sunshine.

CLIA

Then gather some figs. And collect some honey.

AMARYLLIS

I want to hear the news, too. What's the latest in Sparta? How's Helen settling down?

CLIA

Will you do as I tell you?

AMARYLLIS

I'll get the sandals for him. He has big feet, hasn't he? He's not so old, either.

CLIA

(Rising to her feet and turning on AMARYLLIS*)*
I want figs and I want honey.

AMARYLLIS

(Backing toward the door)
Yes, ma'am.

CLIA

That's better. And if I catch you talking to one of those men again, I'll—I'll shave your hair off.

AMARYLLIS

(Runs to the door, and then halts as she sees HOMER*)*

I'm going to gather some figs. Like to help me? You could watch the path to the mountain just as well, out there.

HOMER

I don't need to watch the path any longer. They've started climbing up through the trees. They *actually* mean to hunt a deer! I take that as a sign. A deer means a banquet, a banquet means a contest. They've accepted Penelope's plan.

CLIA
(Carrying the basin of water to the door)
Is that good or bad?
(AMARYLLIS departs hurriedly.)

HOMER
(Moving back into the Hall, as CLIA empties the basin)
It will be good for the next two or three hours, anyway.
(He looks round the silent Hall.)
Peace... This is the way a house should live. I think I'll try to catch some sleep. Nothing very much can happen until those barbarians get back. Call me then. Penelope will need me.
(He has walked over to the steps, and is about to ascend them to the dais. He yawns.)
Yes, sleep's the thing. Sleep... Sleep that knits up the ravelled sleeve of care.

CLIA
(Replacing the basin on its peg)
That's the wrong way! The men sleep through there!
(She points to the door of the men's quarters.)

HOMER

(Retracing his steps, and now headed in the right direction)

Stupid of me! I must be getting as absent-minded as my pupils say. Yet, what is absent-mindedness? A mere forgetting of unimportant things like doors. And what's amusing you, Noman?

ULYSSES

It's a useful kind of forgetting when it leads you into the women's quarters.

HOMER

We aren't all hunters, my friend. Besides, with all this newfangled nonsense of bedrooms, why shouldn't I forget? This is the only house I know which is built this way. Just show me a ridge of mountains, black-pointed against a sunset, or a rosy-fingered dawn caressing a laughing sea, and I'll remember *them*. A door is a door is a door.

(He pauses at the correct door.)

Waken me if any trouble starts.

(He goes out.)

ULYSSES

I believe the old boy would flail around with a sword if he had to... You know, Clia, that's the kind of courage I really admire.

(CLIA has come over to him. She falls on her knees and kisses his sleeve.)

No, no!

(He raises her, gives her a hug, and wipes her eyes with
his hand.)

Besides, don't *you* start forgetting. I'm a beggar. That's how I've come home.

(He stands erect, suddenly, and throws back his cloak.
His hand closes over the dagger at his belt as he looks
at the threshold.)

A beggar, lying hidden in a filthy hut with the smell of pigs around me, plodding through dry hot dust under a full sun, grovelling in front of my own door, being shoved aside and swallowing each insult with a cringing smile...watching my wife's smiles for two men who—

(He curses them under his breath.)

CLIA
(Moving toward the steps, at the mention of PENELOPE*)*
I'll tell her you've come back. Let me break the news gently. The shock would be too great if you suddenly walked into her room.

ULYSSES
(Bitterly)
Yes, let's spare her all unpleasant surprises.

CLIA
Ulysses!

ULYSSES
(Gesturing silence)
Sh!

CLIA

(Dropping her voice obediently, but still shocked)

Have you come back as a beggar to spy on your wife? Then shame on *you*! She has waited *so* long... She has wept and watched—

ULYSSES

(Grimly)

As she did today?

(He takes CLIA by the wrist and pulls her back from the steps.)

CLIA

Let me go! I must tell her. Why, she'll never recognise you like this. I was your nurse, I brought you up, and if it hadn't been for that scar on your leg, I'd never have known you.

ULYSSES

I wish you had known me, as I stood there at the door. Then there could have been an excuse for Penelope and what she did. For a moment, I almost thought she did recognise me...

CLIA

But who would expect you to arrive here as a *beggar*?

ULYSSES

Did you expect me to walk in here and face eleven men with only a dagger at my waist?

CLIA

(Shakes her head, bewildered by everything)

We've talked so often about your home-coming, but never did I imagine anything like this.

ULYSSES

Careful! My home is far away—in Thessaly. Got that? And my name is Noman. My luck ran out in Sparta, and I'm heading home to my own mountains where I hunted as a boy. And I'll live with my daughter, who's married to a drunkard with thirteen children. That's in Thessaly, remember?

CLIA

My, I was getting all ready to weep for you, crowded into a hut with thirteen children. Go on!

(She nudges him playfully.)

You're the same old Ulyss—

(She clamps her own hand this time across her lips.)

ULYSSES

See how easy it is to let the wrong word slip? So, keep quiet. And trust me.

CLIA

But what are you going to do?

ULYSSES

(Laughing as he gives her shoulder an encouraging pat)

First, we reconnoitre. Next, we estimate the situation. And then—we take appropriate action.

CLIA

My! You learned a lot in the army.
(Her hand goes to silence her lips again.)

ULYSSES

Stop thinking of me as Ulysses, will you? Now—
(He is suddenly serious.)
eleven men... The servants have left, they haven't come back?
(CLIA shakes her head.)
As I wandered in here, I noted five men waiting at the stables,
four men down by the stream. Was that accidental?

CLIA

Accidental?

ULYSSES

Do they usually split into two groups?

CLIA

Now that you mention it—I believe they do. Recently, anyway.

ULYSSES

Eryx—that's the fellow with the red hair? He's the leader of
one group?

CLIA

Penelope never did like Eryx. He's too crafty.

ULYSSES

She didn't, did she? What about Melas?

CLIA

You've got it the wrong way round—he's the one who likes her!
You saw that, didn't you?

ULYSSES

(Grimly)

Yes, I saw that. He's the one who fancied the master's chair.

CLIA

(Startled)

Who was to stop him? He's the best fighter of them all!

ULYSSES

(Catching control of himself)

…Yes…who was to stop him?

*(He speaks almost to himself. He strikes his left palm
with his clenched right fist, and turns away from* CLIA.*)*

Were they in the war?

CLIA

Too young for that. They said.

ULYSSES

No military training, then. Good. What about the weapons I
left here? Have they been stolen?

CLIA

Philetius made Telemachus hide them. You remember Philetius?

ULYSSES

I've forgotten no one, Clia.

CLIA

It's been *so* long...

ULYSSES

It's been too long. I see that now.

(*He begins to walk around the Hall, looking at it. He takes a deep breath, almost a sigh.*)

You'll laugh at me, Clia, but when I used to dream of getting back, I thought that all I had to do was to walk into this house, relax by that fire, and be master of my own home.

(*He looks down at his cloak.*)

I'm a clown, all right... Let Homer sing about that!

CLIA

If he lives to do any more singing! If any of us live through this night!... Tell me, where are your men? Are they waiting in the village, until they get a signal from you?

ULYSSES

No. None came back. Some found death in the sea, some stayed—

(PENELOPE *opens the door onto the dais, and stands there.*
ULYSSES *drops his cloak around him and slouches.*)

CLIA

None? But that's terrible—terrible!

PENELOPE

*(Speaking as she comes down into the Hall and goes
over to the doorway, as if enjoying the sunshine in the
yard)*

And what's so terrible?... It's a lovely day. Not a storm cloud
to be seen over the mountains; and here, it is quiet. What's so
terrible?

CLIA

*(Quickly, as she hurries over to the fireplace, and fills
a bowl with soup)*

He was telling me about his daughter—in Thessaly—a drunkard.
I mean, she's married to a drunkard. With thirteen children.
Imagine that!

PENELOPE

(Still studying the view)

Then her husband never went off to any war.

CLIA

*(Carrying the bowl of soup to the table, and setting it
down in front of the master's chair)*

Over here!

*(ULYSSES, who has been watching PENELOPE as she
stands at the door, comes to life and crosses over to
the table.)*

PENELOPE

(Turning round)

Why, Clia, haven't you given our guest something to eat and

drink? What's wrong with you today? And see where you have set the bowl!

(To ULYSSES, *sharply, as he sits down in front of the bowl)*
That is my husband's chair.

ULYSSES
(Rising quickly, moving to a side bench)
...Sorry, ma'am. I didn't know.

CLIA
(Angry)
Yes, that's the master's chair. That's why Melas tries to sit there. And *he's* allowed, often enough.

PENELOPE
(Amused)
Allowed?

(To ULYSSES*)*
He hasn't your good manners. Yes, that's our trouble. It's easy to deal with someone who has standards like our own. But if he doesn't believe in our standards? Then it's little use saying to him: "Look, no honourable man behaves in this way." He only answers—if he bothers to answer—"But *I* behave in this way!" And that's that. So what can we do?

ULYSSES
(Eating the soup hungrily)
You can't argue with men like that, ma'am. All you can do is outfight them. Or outwit them.

(He reaches for the loaf that CLIA *sets beside him.)*

PENELOPE

Then you agree I haven't done so badly? I've managed to keep those men arguing for three years.

(ULYSSES pauses in pouring out some wine. PENELOPE now uses a little irony.)

I couldn't fight them, of course; but why didn't I think of trying to outwit them? How stupid of me! I might even have allowed Melas to sit in my husband's chair so that the others would learn to hate him. Or I could always have used a special smile for Eryx, just to stir up suspicion and jealousy. Oh, *why* didn't I think of such things?

(ULYSSES stops drinking, and sets the goblet down. But as PENELOPE comes slowly nearer to him, he begins eating again—hurriedly, with embarrassment.)

Tell me, what's the news? We don't have many travellers visiting us, nowadays.

ULYSSES

Sorry, ma'am—I don't think you should come too near me. I've been sleeping in rough places. This cloak is filthy.

PENELOPE

Have you heard nothing about my husband—Ulysses?

ULYSSES

They say he's dead. I'm sorry, but that's what they say.

PENELOPE

(To CLIA)

You see! Then why shouldn't I choose another husband?

CLIA

And marry a man you don't love?

PENELOPE

He could be a man who loves me. That is better than no man at all.

(ULYSSES *starts eating, slowly now, as* PENELOPE *watches him. He says nothing.*)

CLIA

But that isn't how you feel!

PENELOPE

If you were I, how would you feel?
                (*She speaks to* ULYSSES.)
You have travelled and seen many women. Tell me—am I too old to marry?

ULYSSES

No.

PENELOPE

Am I too ugly?

ULYSSES

No.

PENELOPE

Wouldn't you say—as a man who has learned a lot about life in his travels—that this house needs a master? Or that my son needs a father's advice? He's almost eighteen now, you know.

(ULYSSES *is silent.* PENELOPE *turns away, speaking as if to herself.*)

Or that I need love, like any other woman?

(ULYSSES *pushes away the bowl of soup and drops the hunk of bread on the table.* PENELOPE *walks slowly to the centre of the Hall.*)

If Ulysses were alive—but he isn't. He can't be, or he surely would have sent some messages to me during those long, long years. Wouldn't he? Look at me! Am I the kind of woman who is so easily forgotten?

(*She faces him.* ULYSSES *rises abruptly, and walks toward the door.*)

ULYSSES

Thank you for the food, ma'am.

PENELOPE

Are you leaving? So soon?

(ULYSSES *halts, almost at the door, as if trying to control himself.*)

CLIA

He's got worries of his own. Stop pestering the man! He has nowhere to go, don't you see? And he's travelled far.

(*Poor* CLIA *is at the stage of wringing her hands.*)

PENELOPE

(*To* ULYSSES)

Then why not stay here, for tonight at least? I shan't bother you any more with my troubles. But I'll give you news to take on your journey.

(Her voice rises.)

Tonight, I'll choose a husband. *That* story will buy you many a free meal on your travels.

(She begins to laugh.)

CLIA

Oh, Penelope! How cruel you are!

PENELOPE

Cruel? Who has been cruel?

(Suddenly, she turns and runs to the steps. Her laughter has changed to weeping. ULYSSES stares after her. PENELOPE halts with her foot on the first step.)

Oh, help me! Athena!

(ATHENA appears on the dais, and she stands there, looking down on PENELOPE.)

ATHENA

Careful, now! You are doing very nicely. But don't get emotional, or you'll spoil your plan.

PENELOPE

I can't go on with it, I *can't*—

(She turns and looks at ULYSSES, brushing away her tears. He stands very erect, now, watching her.)

ATHENA

Penelope, *think*!... Oh—
(*She throws up her hands helplessly as* PENELOPE *runs to* ULYSSES, *who has suddenly held open his arms.*)
—Penelope!

PENELOPE

Ulysses, Ulysses!

ULYSSES

(*Catching her in his arms, looking at her. He throws his hat aside, and drops his cloak.*)
Penelope...
(*He kisses her passionately.*)

ATHENA

Oh, you human beings! No wonder your lives get so muddled.
(*She walks down the steps and across the Hall to the large doorway.*)
When will you learn wisdom? But then—I suppose it isn't so much fun to be wise.
(*She looks at them as she passes by, and sighs as she watches a long kiss.*)
It must be fun to be human, just once in a while...
(*She suddenly halts, almost at the threshold.*)
And now I'm losing *my* wits. I'm still needed here. After all the trouble I've had in bringing Ulysses home, I'm not going to leave this job half-done. Look at them! At this moment they haven't a thought between them. Here, you two! Enough's enough. Snap out of it!

(She claps her hands sharply together, and then retires into the background, composes herself to wait, and becomes quite motionless.)

ULYSSES

(Holding PENELOPE *suddenly away from him)*

You little devil! That was a fine performance to tear a man's heart out. Was that the idea—tear it out, then jump on it with both feet?

(But he is laughing. Suddenly he becomes serious.)

When did you recognise me? Or was it Eumaeus who let you know I had come home?

PENELOPE

(Evasively)

He didn't *tell* me.

ULYSSES

(Letting her go)

Then, when did you know me?

PENELOPE

Don't you mean how did I know you?

ULYSSES

(Angry)

I don't mean *how,* I mean *when.*

(Catching her by her wrists)

When?

PENELOPE

Oh, Clia, he really *does* love me!... Darling, darling, I knew all along that the beggar was you. Now, don't blame Eumaeus. I just sort of extracted the news from him. And besides, why did you hide it from me?

(ULYSSES *is silent.*)

When I came into the Hall this afternoon and found Eryx and Melas here, I had to play for time. And suddenly, suddenly I saw you at the door—oh, Ulysses, you made the most beggarly beggar I ever saw! Then I knew it was quite safe to announce the contest.

ULYSSES

Safe, was it?

PENELOPE

But don't you see—you are *bound* to win! Only you know how to manage that Great Bow. And remember, I said the contest was open to everyone in the Hall tonight. Don't I get a kiss for being clever?

ULYSSES

(*Looks at the Great Bow and then says quietly*)

Why had there to be a contest?

PENELOPE

I was forced to do *something*. You saw that.

ULYSSES

Why are the men still here? They were leaving this morning. If they had, there would have been no need for any contest.

(PENELOPE *tries to evade his eyes, but he turns her face*
toward his.)

What kept them here?

PENELOPE
(Dejectedly)

I did.

ULYSSES
(Watching her carefully)

Why?... Did you play with the idea of marrying Melas?

PENELOPE
(Angry)

No! Nor Eryx. Nor any of the others.
(More quietly)

I—I kept them here only after I knew you were coming home.

ULYSSES
(Slowly)

Did you hate me so much?

PENELOPE

No—oh, don't you see?

ULYSSES

Frankly, I don't.

PENELOPE

Oh, there were so many reasons. But chiefly—chiefly—

ULYSSES

Yes?

PENELOPE
(Quickly)

You wouldn't want those men to escape from here, without paying for what they have done. Would you? After all, the Hero of the Trojan War doesn't just come home and, and—

ULYSSES

The Hero of the Trojan War only wanted to come home and relax with his wife and son.

PENELOPE

Then why didn't the Hero of the Trojan War come home when the last battle was won?

ULYSSES

So this mess is all *my* fault, is it?
(PENELOPE *pulls her hands free and covers her face to hide her tears. He draws her gently to him.)*
And so it is... I'm sorry, Penelope... Forgive me.

PENELOPE

(Throwing her arms around him again)

Oh, Ulysses... Can you forgive me?

(The curtain closes swiftly.)

SCENE 2

There has been a short passage of time: the same characters are still in the Hall. Only, PENELOPE *is now sitting on* ULYSSES' *knees, and he sits in his chair. They are both talking, explaining, while poor* ATHENA *sits on one of the broad steps and sleeps,* CLIA, *her back turned tactfully, has dozed off, too, by the hearth. (The slant of the sunshine coming in through the main entrance has altered; but the shadow has not yet reached the mark that* ERYX *had scored on the floor.)* TELEMACHUS *enters, and halts just inside the door, amazed,* ULYSSES *immediately jumps to his feet, swinging* PENELOPE *behind him, and draws his dagger as he faces the door,* ATHENA *is jolted awake.*

ULYSSES

(Furious)

Sweet suffering Jupiter! Don't do that to me, boy! I thought it was one of those bastards sneaking in.

(CLIA is awake, too, now.)

TELEMACHUS

Sorry, Father, I really am.

(He comes forward nervously, and then beams with delight.)

But I'm glad you told Mother who you are.

PENELOPE

I would have probably found out, anyway.

TELEMACHUS

Oh no, you wouldn't. His disguise was cool, it really was.

ULYSSES

(Sheathes his dagger and smiles)

Well, we shan't argue about that. Where's Eumaeus?

TELEMACHUS

Just outside.

(He whistles and EUMAEUS shambles in.)

We did what you told us. We—

ULYSSES

(Quickly)

Good, good. And where is Philetius?

TELEMACHUS

He'll be out in the stables.

ULYSSES

Bring him here.

TELEMACHUS

Yes, sir!

(He runs into the yard.)

PENELOPE

What on earth was Telemachus trying to say? *We did what you told us?*

ULYSSES

Oh, they were just helping to strengthen my will power. Well, it's good to know that Philetius got safely home.

PENELOPE

(Still thinking of TELEMACHUS*)*

But, darling, what did they—

ULYSSES

The last time I saw him, we were out on a raid together—a night raid on the Trojan camp.

(As he speaks, TELEMACHUS *enters with a thin man of about fifty. This is* PHILETIUS. *He comes to attention when he sees* ULYSSES. *But* ULYSSES *catches him in a rough bear hug.)*

Philetius, you old rascal, you old ruffian…

(To the others)

He was the best god-damned sergeant I ever had.
(He thumps PHILETIUS *on the back, but he can't go on
speaking.)*

TELEMACHUS

Philetius?... And what's a night raid?

ULYSSES

Just an idea I worked out—and the opposition I got at first from
the high brass! Roughly, a night raid was this: we blackened
our faces, crawled on our bellies, silenced the sentries, took a
couple of prisoners for information. And then, we got the hell
out.

(Laughing)

Don't look so shocked, Telemachus. Isn't it heroic enough
for you? But it's the way to win a war. All that old-fashioned
business of having duels between opposing generals—bah!
Nothing was ever decided that way. As soon as a general got
killed in a duel, then another officer was promoted to be a
general. And of course he wanted to have a duel, too. Big stuff,
you know—both armies watching, publicity, applause. It goes
to a man's head, that sort of thing. And the war just never got
finished. Now, my idea was to win, to win as thoroughly and
quickly as possible, and let the men get home.

(At the last word, he glances quickly over at PENELOPE.
He looks embarrassed and rubs his head.)

Yes, yes. Go on! Say it!

PENELOPE
(Smiling a little)
We were out on a night raid, weren't we?

ULYSSES
(Grinning)
So we were... Actually, we were coming back from a raid. Philetius was covering our withdrawal. He was a good man with a knife—eh, Philetius?
(PHILETIUS smiles.)
But, that night, he was captured. The Trojans questioned him.
(PHILETIUS nods.)
He told them nothing, except his name, rank, and number.
(PHILETIUS shakes his head in agreement.)
So after a week of various persuasions, they lost their temper and tore out his tongue. They made him a slave in a mill, but when Troy went up in flames, he escaped. Right, Philetius?
(PHILETIUS nods.)

TELEMACHUS
(Looking at PHILETIUS with awe)
But, Father, how did you find out all that?

ULYSSES
Some of our best spies were Trojans... Now, let's get back to our own little war. Eumaeus, Philetius, Telemachus, myself. Against eleven men.

PENELOPE

But darling—you won't have to do *any* fighting! You are going to win the contest.

ULYSSES

I'd just as soon have some friends to back me up, when I do. Eumaeus—keep your eyes on that hillside, will you? I'd like some warning before these men do get back.

(EUMAEUS *moves out into the yard.*)

PENELOPE

Let's have no extra trouble, darling. Please! All you have to do is to win. Those men are cowards—that's why they are so bold. When they see how strong you are, they'll melt into the night like shadows on a hillside.

ULYSSES

They may need a little help in melting. Now, an arrow through each throat might do it. But that's a long job.

(He *walks over to the door as he talks and looks up at the bow.*)

Can you manage it, old friend? Or shall we settle for one clean swift arrow through Melas, and another one through Eryx? The rest of them might argue less, after that.

(He *reaches up his hand and strokes the bow.*)

I'd like just to have the feel of you again. It's been a long time.

(He *lifts the bow down and raises it into holding position, the unstrung bow at arm's full length in front of him, his arm straight and rigid.*)

When I was a boy, Telemachus, I had to stand like this for an hour each day. That's the way my father taught me to strengthen my arm.

TELEMACHUS

(Glumly)

You mean I've got to stand like that for an hour, every day?

ULYSSES

If you want to master this bow. It's more powerful than you think.

(He relaxes his arm, rubs its muscles, and then unwinds the bow's string. He kneels on his right knee, holding the bow in a scissor-grip between his legs—one horn resting over his right thigh, the other clamped under his left thigh. Now he sits back on his right heel as he presses the horns up toward him, recurving them. It is a mighty effort. But not enough: the string, attached to the tip of the right horn, refuses to meet the tip of the left horn. He pulls and forces. His arm trembles with the strain.)

In Athena's name! What's gone wrong? This damned bow—

(ATHENA, who has been inconspicuous in the background, comes quietly forward. ULYSSES is still trying to string the bow. His hand slips and he almost falls with the bow's spring.)

Hell and—

ATHENA

Blood pressure, blood pressure! Don't take it so hard, Ulysses. After all, you haven't handled a bow like that for seventeen years.

ULYSSES

This old bow is stiff with age!

PENELOPE

Try again, darling! You must, you *must*! Try again!

ULYSSES

(Wrestling with the bow)

All I need is practice. Give me time.

PENELOPE

(Frantic, now)

But we haven't *got* time—

ATHENA

Keep out of this, my sweet! Didn't I try to stop you from announcing the contest until we saw how Ulysses could handle this bow? You and your bright ideas!

PENELOPE

—oh, oh, what have I done?

(She bursts into tears. TELEMACHUS is horrified. CLIA is as upset as PENELOPE. PHILETIUS stands, helpless.)

ULYSSES

(Holds the bow away from him. He wipes his brow and stares at it. He speaks very quietly.)

What the hell has happened to me?

ATHENA

We don't get any younger.

(Her voice becomes stronger as ULYSSES *covers his eyes with his hands. The others stare at* ULYSSES *as if transfixed.)*

Now, keep cool, Ulysses. We've been in some bad spots before this. In the last seventeen years, you and I have thought our way out of many a tight corner.

*(*ULYSSES *drops his hand, lifts the bow, and places it back on the wall. Then he turns and looks at* PENELOPE.*)*

ULYSSES

Well, old girl? There's your Hero of the Trojan War.

(He begins to laugh, not altogether with amusement.)

PENELOPE

(Running to him)

I don't want any hero. I just want Ulysses.

(She kisses him.)

I'm less afraid of you, just as you are. Oh darling… All you need is some practice with the bow. If you just could get an hour alone with it…

ULYSSES

(Nodding)

An hour would do it. I hope.

*(*EUMAEUS *whistles a warning from the yard.)*

But we don't even get that…

EUMAEUS

(Appearing at the door)

One man, coming down the mountainside.

(He looks back at the mountain.)

ULYSSES
(Puzzled)

Only one?

EUMAEUS
(Standing at one side of the door, his eyes still watching)

No one is following him, as yet... He's alone. Hurrying, too.
But he's still some distance from the road.

PENELOPE

Then we still have some time before he reaches here.
*(Quickly, as the men look at each other, their hands
now on their daggers)*

I've an idea—

(ATHENA covers her eyes.)

ULYSSES
(In mock alarm)

Another one?

PENELOPE

Quick, Clia—pack some food. Telemachus, get the water skins.
Carry them down to the Bay. I'll get some blankets.
*(She is moving toward the steps to her room, as ULYSSES
speaks to her.)*

ULYSSES

Are we going camping or something?

PENELOPE

Darling, have you forgotten? We have our boat in the Bay.

TELEMACHUS

But we can't! We can't sail—

PENELOPE

Of course we can. It takes five men to sail that boat, but now that Ulysses is home we can easily manage it.

TELEMACHUS

But we—

ULYSSES

Let me handle this, old boy.
(To PENELOPE, *gently*)
Darling, we aren't going to run away.

PENELOPE

We aren't running. We are sailing. That's quite different.

ULYSSES

(*Gently*)

We aren't doing either. Because we can't. I gave orders for a little persuasion to be used on our boat—with a hammer and chisel.

PENELOPE

On *our* boat?

TELEMACHUS

That's what I've been trying to tell you. It will split wide open as soon as it's out of the Bay. It will never last in open waters.

(Grins for ULYSSES*)*

We did a good job, all right. You wouldn't notice the damage unless you went looking for it.

ULYSSES

The boat was just too tempting, Penelope. I saw it, as I came here today. And I found myself thinking about it—*and* the mainland. When a man starts thinking about retreat, he is already beaten.

EUMAEUS

(Reporting from the door, where he stands, watching vigilantly)

He has reached the road now. Running his horse pretty hard. It's Eryx. I can see his hair glint in the sun, as hot as a beacon. Ah, ah!—Some more are beginning to move down the mountainside!

ULYSSES

(Catching PENELOPE *by the arm, urging her up the steps to her doorway)*

Into your room. Stay there. Keep out of sight.

PENELOPE

But—

ULYSSES

Keep *out* of sight! Stay away from this Hall!

PENELOPE
(Resisting, unwilling, worried)

But darling—what will you do?

ULYSSES

Practise.

PENELOPE

With the bow?
*(From the distance comes the sound of a galloping
horse)*

There isn't time—

ULYSSES
(Gives her a quick hug)

Leave that to me.
*(He adds a smack on her bottom and sends her running
up the steps.)*

And lock the door to your room!
(PENELOPE leaves obediently.)

ATHENA

That's right, master. Let her know who is the boss around
here. You've won your first battle, Ulysses. And what about
the next one?
*(ULYSSES has swung round to face the door, his hand
ready on his dagger. TELEMACHUS and PHILETIUS have
come to stand beside him. EUMAEUS, still watching the
yard, pulls his body out of sight from anyone who may
be arriving there. The beat of hoofs is strong, then*

silenced as if someone were dismounting.)

Shall we play it easy—wait until we see why Eryx is in such a hurry?

(ULYSSES relaxes a little.)

TELEMACHUS

But when can you practise with the bow?

ULYSSES

We'll practise a little deception, first.

(He picks up the cloak, draws it around him, and retreats to the fireplace bench.)

TELEMACHUS

Aren't you going to deal with Eryx?

(He looks at the door and then at his unsheathed knife. But PHILETIUS, at a sign from ULYSSES, puts his arm around the boy's shoulder, and shakes his head. TELEMACHUS walks over to the table, disconsolately, and sits on its edge. PHILETIUS, at another quick sign from ULYSSES, sits on one of the steps leading to the dais and begins to whittle. CLIA is preparing some food for a soup pot, and she is using her largest knife. All watch the door.)

EUMAEUS

(Bowing to the yard with a deep flourish and speaking mockingly)

Welcome, my lord, welcome!

(ERYX enters, hurriedly. He takes in the Hall with a glance, and seems reassured.)

You had a fast ride. I think you've ruined your horse.

ERYX

(To CLIA*)*

Get a blanket and a couple of poles.

(To the others)

Take them up the mountain. Help is needed. Get a move on, there!

ULYSSES

A stretcher case? Now, isn't that too bad? I hope it isn't Melas.

ERYX

A rock fell on a couple of men. One of them is badly hurt.

ULYSSES

But not Melas. How disappointing for you.

ERYX

(Shouting)

Get a move on, I tell you!

(But no one moves. ERYX *notices the knife in* PHILETIUS' *hand, still whittling; and the knife in* CLIA'S *hand, now chopping vegetables with determination; and the knife that telemachus is using to carve an initial in the corner of the table.* ERYX'S *hand goes to the sword at his waist, and he backs to the door, keeping an eye on all these knives.)*

ULYSSES

You'd like us all to clear out so that you could have this Hall to yourself, would you? If you were thinking of trying out the Great Bow, then go ahead. Who's stopping you? Melas is still up on the mountain with the injured man, isn't he?

ERYX

(Pulling his sword)

Who are you?

ULYSSES

(Rising, standing astride on the hearth, but still keeping
his cloak around him)

Yes, it all makes a pretty picture. A hunting party scattered
on a mountainside. A crag suddenly plunges down. It misses
Melas, but gets two of his friends who were standing beside
him. Up comes Eryx, the ever-useful. "I'll ride for help," he says.
Obliging fellow. And before the others have gathered their wits,
such as they are, Eryx is halfway down the mountain. He keeps
his word, too: tries to get us all out of here, carrying first aid up
the mountain. Most touching. But we are not going, Eryx.

ERYX

(Taking a stand, raising his sword, but watching the
knives around him which now have stopped whittling,
chopping, and carving)

Who are you?

ULYSSES

Just a man who wants to see you smuggle a shot or two with that
bow, so that you can win tonight. That's your idea, isn't it?…

(He laughs.)

You're a clever lad, Eryx; and like all clever lads, you'd be none
the worse of a hanging.

(His voice changes.)

Put up that sword! If we had wanted to, we could have slit

your throat by this time and dropped you, tied to an anchor, into the Bay.

ERYX

Then why don't you?

ULYSSES

Why take the trouble? You'll be killed together, all eleven of you.

ERYX
(Pretending to be amused, but watchful)
Will we? You know... I kind of admire your impudence. Who are you, anyway?
(EUMAEUS gives a warning whistle, and ERYX notices that
TELEMACHUS, PHILETIUS, *and* CLIA *look anxiously toward*
the door.)
Yes, listen to that warning. There's your reason for not slitting my throat. You are afraid of my friends who are now riding down from the mountain.

EUMAEUS

Not all of them, Eryx. There's only a small band coming down. And they're riding in a normal way—just a slow easy trot.
(The information is more for ULYSSES *than for* ERYX.
The others look to ULYSSES *for his command, and* ERYX
notices this. He speaks worriedly.)

ERYX

WHO ARE YOU?

ULYSSES

You are inclined to repeat yourself, aren't you?

(He throws aside the cloak, over his shoulders.)

All right. I was sent here by Ulysses. I'm a captain in his forces.
We landed last night, on the north shore of the island. Forty-
three men, and Ulysses himself.

ERYX

Ulysses?

ULYSSES

He entered the village this morning. The people have decided
they are on our side, after all. And so have some of your
servants—the few who survived.

(He is grinning broadly, speaking confidently.)

So we've got the whole of the island, except for this southern corner.
And Ulysses is tightening the net around it, minute by minute.

ERYX

(Trying to regain his own confidence)

A likely story!

ULYSSES

Tell that to Ulysses when you see him. Just after sunset, in fact.
Won't be long, now.

ERYX

(Sneering, but taking a step backward)

Ulysses sent you, his captain, to walk in here and be cut down
by eleven men!

ULYSSES

(Equably)

I walked in here to tell Penelope that help is coming. I'm staying here to guard this Hall. It's defensible. That's the way Ulysses built it.

(He moves quickly to the steps, and stands in front of them, dagger drawn. PHILETIUS *rises, his knife ready.* TELEMACHUS *circles round to join them.)*

All we have to do is to tie you up, bar the double doors, and wait for Ulysses and his men. Telemachus, we'll need four swords, a couple of spears, some throwing knives. Quick!

(To ERYX, *again)*

Did you think we had no weapons at all? Now, don't harm the boy unless you want to die in a very unpleasant fashion. Ulysses has a nasty temper, and a long memory.

*(*ERYX *hesitates in attacking* TELEMACHUS, *and the boy slips out into the yard.)*

EUMAEUS

(Still watching at the door)

Yes, your friends are taking their time, Eryx. And I don't see Melas among them.

ULYSSES

How many?

EUMAEUS

Five of them—four together, and one straggling.

ULYSSES

(To ERYX *as he backs toward the door)*

Stay here, Eryx, stay here... It wouldn't be any good warning them. Ulysses controls the village. Even if you could fight your way to the harbour, you'd find no escape there. The ships have all been sent away. And this, let me remind you, is an island. It's a long, long swim to the mainland.

ERYX

(Wary)

Ulysses sent the ships away? And they left, obediently?

(He begins to smile.)

That's a big order for forty-three men to enforce. You've been too clever, Captain... I nearly believed your story. But that last touch!

(He begins to laugh, his sword is raised.)

You'd be none the worse of a hanging, yourself.

ULYSSES

(Smiling broadly)

The ships all left. For the mainland. Where they will pick up the booty that we brought back from the war. You're right: forty-three men might not have been enough to empty a harbour, but seventeen years of collectors' items roused a lot of curiosity. And it isn't junk that's lying over on the wharves of Ragusa, waiting for us to load it and bring it here. It isn't a Trojan shield, or a broken sword, or an arrowhead or two. It's a few mementos from palaces, in gold and pearls and silver; and some reminders of our visit to Circe's island; and some gifts from Calypso; and a few odds and ends we liberated from the Cyclops' cave. Enough—enough for all of us, and for the people who help us. You'd be surprised how quickly they volunteered to sail to Ragusa.

ERYX

(As the sound of walking horses and jingling harness
at last is heard)

One move from any of you—and a shout from me will bring them at a gallop.

(He thrusts EUMAEUS *aside, and straddles the doorway*
with his drawn sword.)

Try barring the door, Captain!

(He smiles in triumph.)

But, at least, we can now talk. I think we understand each other. You want to live to collect your share of the loot, and marry a pretty girl and settle down. I've no objection to that.

ULYSSES

(Ironically)

That's very civil of you.

ERYX

And I'm a man who knows when to cut his losses. If the game goes against me, I stop playing.

ULYSSES

So what's your bargain?

ERYX

I won't kill you—

ULYSSES

Like to try?

ERYX

—and I won't denounce you to the others. I'll leave you to play
the beggar until Ulysses gets here.

ULYSSES

And the other side of the bargain?

ERYX

You'll let me leave this island.

ULYSSES

But Ulysses may not agree to that.

ERYX

I shan't stay to argue with Ulysses.

ULYSSES

But there's no escape by the harbour.

ERYX

I'll do my own planning. Well—is the bargain made?
        (He catches EUMAEUS suddenly, twisting the old man in
                front of him as a shield.)
Do I yell for the others?
        (The voices of men are now heard faintly from the
                courtyard.)
Or do I leave you in peace—and you leave me in peace?

ULYSSES

...I agree. You'll never slip through our line of men anyway...
All right! I said I agreed. Take your sword out of his back!

ERYX

And not a word to Melas?

ULYSSES

I said I agreed.

> (TELEMACHUS *enters, carrying an armful of weapons.*
> *He has a quiver, with a few arrows, slung over his*
> *shoulder. He halts. He stares in amazement.)*

Stand aside, Telemachus.

> (ERYX *lets* EUMAEUS *free, and moves quickly into the*
> *yard.)*

TELEMACHUS

You let him *go?*

> (ULYSSES *raises a warning hand. They all stand silent.*
> *But there is no yell from outside.* EUMAEUS, *rubbing his*
> *shoulder, goes to the door again.)*

EUMAEUS

He's strolling down toward the stream as cool as grass.

TELEMACHUS

That's where the others went to water their horses. I had to
wait until they couldn't see me across the yard. And I came too
late... I even brought you some arrows for the bow, all I could
find that weren't broken. There are only four of them...

*(He dumps the weapons in a pile at his feet, and pushes
them disgustedly with his foot.)*

Why agree with Eryx? You can't trust him.

ULYSSES

I can trust him to be himself. Philetius, slip out and take the
short cut to the road into the village. Choose a couple of
throwing-knives to keep you company. I want you to guard
the road, just at the crest of the hill from which you can see
the harbour. No one is to reach that crest. No one is to see the
harbour. No one is to report back here to Eryx. Got that?

*(PHILETIUS has moved over to the heap of weapons, and
chosen two knives which he weighs for a moment in
his hands and then slips into his belt. As ULYSSES asks his
question, he nods and picks up a third knife, to throw
at the wall, where it strikes and holds. CLIA exclaims.
TELEMACHUS' mouth falls open. PHILETIUS pauses as he is
about to leave by the door, and points across the Hall
to the doorway of the men's quarters.)*

You're right. Better leave by a window from that side of the
house.

*(PHILETIUS has already moved to that doorway. He goes
out. ULYSSES advances on the heap of weapons.)*

Now, let's get this cleared away.

*(He lifts a sword and pushes it through his belt, and
starts carrying the rest of the weapons to the nearest
chest. It lies against the wall, between the steps to
the dais and the fireplace. CLIA helps him. TELEMACHUS
selects a sword for himself.)*

Come on, Telemachus. Hide that sword. Meanwhile...

TELEMACHUS
(Puts it unwillingly inside the chest, as ULYSSES *pulls the*
knife from the wall and throws it into the chest, too)

I just don't know anything, that's the trouble. Every time something happens, I'm not there. I just don't know *anything*.

ULYSSES
(Thinking; then pulling out the sword he had chosen
and adding it to the chest)

Painful, but necessary. We'll keep our daggers—even a beggar can own a knife without causing suspicion.

(He begins to help CLIA *stuff back the linen from the*
chest on top of the weapons. They close the chest.)

That's right, Clia; put pots and pans on top. You're preparing a banquet. Remember?

CLIA
Banquet!

(She sniffs.)

ULYSSES
In case they stay to dinner—how's the wine?

CLIA
We are down to our last barrel.

ULYSSES
Then strengthen it. I want one cup to be as powerful as four. What's wrong? You used to make the drugs and medicines.

CLIA

I was just thinking—what a pity I never specialised in poisons!

ULYSSES

(Putting a couple of bowls on top of the chest for good measure)

No, thank you. You stick to sleeping powders and we'll keep our appetites.

(He has walked back to his place at the hearth, and draws his cloak around him.)

TELEMACHUS

(Looking at his father, then at CLIA, *who has begun to cut up vegetables again, then at* EUMAEUS, *who is still at his post)*

You aren't going to be a beggar again? Aren't we going to fight?

ULYSSES

In our own way. And at our own time. Relax, Telemachus. Try to imagine the touching little scene being played down at the stream, right now. They are still there, Eumaeus?

EUMAEUS

Still there. A lot of talking's going on.

ULYSSES

Eryx is spinning a good story—I wish I could hear him. He is persuading some half-wit to take the hill road into the village.

TELEMACHUS

And Philetius will ambush him!

ULYSSES

You see, I didn't trust Eryx so much. He didn't believe my story altogether. But he will, when his man doesn't come back with a report on the harbour. He'll believe then that Ulysses is in control of the island.

CLIA

Eryx may send more than one man to scout the harbour.

ULYSSES

He may. But that would leave him shorthanded for sailing our boat to the mainland.

TELEMACHUS

He's going to take our boat? Oh, Jupiter!
(He starts for the door.)

ULYSSES

Stay here, boy!

TELEMACHUS

I wouldn't let them *see* me watching them.

ULYSSES

Stay here and forget about it. You've a lot to learn about fighting, haven't you? Battles can be won by courage, but wars are won with brains. Remember that. And remember, too, that a man's a fool who starts a war and doesn't win it. What kind of hero is he then? So wait. That's the first thing you learn in the army—there's always plenty of waiting to do.

CLIA

But Eryx is clever; he might—

ULYSSES

Clever?

(He laughs.)

There's a point where astuteness makes a full circle and meets stupidity. The greatest fools I ever met were those who prided themselves on their cleverness. Let me tell you of the Trojans when they laughed at Cassandra's warning about the Wooden Horse—

(But the door to the men's quarters is opened, and HOMER *comes into the Hall.)*

HOMER

Really, a most remarkable thing! I could swear a man entered my room, entered it silently, not even begging my pardon, crossed to the window, and jumped out. And when I rose, and went to look—nothing. Nothing to be seen. Except quiet fields and sleeping trees, and the waves rolling in to pound themselves to pieces against the cliffs.

(He crosses to the fireplace.)

You don't believe me? I assure you the man seemed as real as you do now. Yet, I stood there at the window and looked and he had—he had melted into air, into thin air.

CLIA

You must have been dreaming.

HOMER

Dreaming? Perhaps... We are such stuff as dreams are made on, and our little life is rounded with a sleep... Hm! I rather like that. I forgive the man, if he can stir up such thoughts to keep me company.
(*To* ULYSSES)
When we are old, our thoughts are our friends.

ULYSSES

Then we'd better choose them carefully. A man is marked by the company he keeps.
(AMARYLLIS *strolls in, carrying a large basket of figs and a respectable-sized pot of honey.*)

CLIA
(*Watching* AMARYLLIS)

Indeed he is.

AMARYLLIS

There!
(*She dumps the basket and pot on the table.*)
Figs. Honey. And that's my job done for the day.

CLIA

I need some—

AMARYLLIS

It's my night off. The sun is just about to set.

HOMER
(Goes over to the mark ERYX *had made on the floor,*
now lying in the shadow)
The men are late. See—they haven't kept their threat!
(He points to the mark, and smiles all around.)

AMARYLLIS
There's a dance in the village tonight, but no one will take me.
Hey, what about you, traveller? Like to go with me? We could
borrow a donkey and—

CLIA
No one will take you to the dance, eh? Have you been talking
to those men again?

AMARYLLIS
I wasn't *talking*. I only asked Lucas to wait and give me a lift.
But he rode off, and left me standing at the stream. And Eryx
turned on me, and I—

HOMER
(Excited)
One moment! All this happened down at the stream? When?

AMARYLLIS
Just before I brought in the figs.
(To CLIA*)*
But I wasn't *talking* to them.

CLIA

It wasn't for lack of trying. Just you wait and I'll—
> (*She drops her work and rushes toward* AMARYLLIS,
> *who escapes quickly into the yard. She returns to the*
> *table, where she has been working.*)

HOMER

Clia, you were much too quick. There's something important in what she says, if only we could understand it. This Lucas person—riding into the village?

ULYSSES

The sacrificial goat.

HOMER

I beg your pardon?

ULYSSES

He'd better take his coat. The evenings turn cold, round here.

HOMER

Your blood is thin, my man. Look, while you've been sitting here, something has developed. These men, or some of them at least, have returned; but they don't come to the Hall! And one of them goes riding off toward the village. Now don't you see—

ULYSSES

Did you get any sleep this afternoon?

HOMER

No. I was too busy thinking about my poem. But don't change the subject! What has been happening here? I felt it as soon as I came into the Hall: I sensed a—a difference. You are all too peaceful, too relaxed.

ULYSSES

I'm not changing any subject. You needed sleep; you didn't get it. Result: nervous and—

HOMER
(Testily)

I am not!

EUMAEUS
(From his lookout post at the door)

If it was all too peaceful for your taste, you can be happy now. Melas and his friends are coming down the mountainside.

ULYSSES

How many?

EUMAEUS

...Four, I make it. Four riders, and five horses.

CLIA
(As HOMER hurries over to the door to look toward the mountain, too)

Where's the fifth man? Did they leave him—?
(She silences her lips with her hands.)

HOMER

(Watching the distance)

Only four men, most definitely.

(ULYSSES lifts a charred piece of wood from the hearth as he rises, and, with a smile for CLIA, he scores one stroke on the wall. He throws the piece of wood into the hearth again, and takes his seat.)

HOMER

(Nervous, as he still watches the distant riders)

I don't like this... Keep calm, Eumaeus! Keep calm!

EUMAEUS

Me?

HOMER

My advice is to forget these men and concentrate on something pleasant, like a—like a sunset. Look at that one, Eumaeus, just beginning. How would you describe the sun? I see it as a winged chariot moving slowly, surely, on its way to the stables of night.

EUMAEUS

It's a wheel of cheese to me, and I wish I had a wedge of it. I haven't eaten since morning.

HOMER

Look at it! It never betrays our trust... What if we were to waken tomorrow morning, and never see it again? Bright sun, would I were steadfast as thou art...

(He wanders, speaking, into the courtyard.)

EUMAEUS

(Watching him)

Now, when *I* go around talking to myself, people say I'm crazy.
It's useful, being a poet.

ULYSSES

(Quickly, to TELEMACHUS*)*

Don't let Homer wander around. Eryx might think he is spying.
Bring him back here, somehow.

(He watches TELEMACHUS *follow* HOMER, *worriedly.)*

I'm afraid Homer won't approve of my way of fighting any
more than Telemachus.

CLIA

*(Who has been filling the wine vases from a barrel of
wine, all this time)*

But Homer has seen you fight before.

ULYSSES

No. He has seen only the results of the way I fight.

CLIA

Well, he always admired *them*.

ATHENA

(Comes to life, and moves over to the frowning ULYSSES*)*

Sleep is what he needs, isn't it? If he woke up only after the
fighting was all over, then he could admire the results once
more. Why add to his worries? He's having trouble enough
with Penelope in his poem. Besides, you don't want the major

poet of Greece to be killed in your house. Let him sleep, and stay out of harm's way.

CLIA

ULYSSES

(To CLIA, *as* ATHENA *touches his shoulder and then walks out through the nearest wall)*

What's that you're mixing with the wine? Something to strengthen it?

(He rises to go over to the table, to watch her work.)

CLIA

If you'd let me add enough, I'd have them all stretched snoring on the floor. You could polish them off, then.

ULYSSES

That isn't killing. That's murder. When I do lift a sword, I fight fair.

CLIA

But the odds against you are heavy.

ULYSSES

I'll take them. The only odds I refuse are the impossible ones.

CLIA

All right, all right... I was only trying to help.

ULYSSES

Then offer Homer a drink. He needs to catch up on his sleep. You are sure that stuff won't harm him?

(He points to the small flask that CLIA *is using very carefully on the wine vases.)*

CLIA

Harm?

(She laughs.)

It's helped Penelope through many a bad night. I used to—

(She breaks off as HOMER *and* TELEMACHUS *enter the Hall.)*

HOMER

(To TELEMACHUS*)*

I *know* the evening dew is treacherous, but I don't think it is liable to fall for a few more hours. The sun isn't even down yet!

(To CLIA*)*

I believe this young man is afraid I'll meet with an accident, out there.

ULYSSES

Could be.

(He wanders around, restlessly.)

HOMER

But Eryx and his friends are much too busy carrying water down to the Bay to worry about me. Now why should they be doing that?

ULYSSES

Perhaps they think the tide's too low.

(He laughs uproariously.)

HOMER

And if I tell you that Melas and his friends are almost here, will you laugh that off, too? And do you know what that extra horse is carrying? A dead man.

ULYSSES

Then I'd say they had run into a spot of trouble. Perhaps met one of your friends, up in that forest.

(He sits on the bench by the table, and faces outward, his back against the table's edge, to watch the door.)

HOMER

One of *my* friends?

ULYSSES

One of those boars you keep talking about.

HOMER

(Losing his impatience, suddenly interested)

Ah, that reminds me—I wanted to tell you my version of a boar hunt. You're a hunter, so you could set me right if I've some details wrong. But what a pity!

ULYSSES

What's the pity?

HOMER

We haven't time!

ULYSSES

What's a better time than this? Eumaeus—leave that door, now.
Come in! Relax!

HOMER

You mean—waiting here, we could—perhaps you are right.
Noman, I believe I owe you an apology.
> *(He starts moving to the fireplace.* ULYSSES *yawns and*
> *stretches;* TELEMACHUS, *glumly, comes forward to the*
> *table;* EUMAEUS *follows him.)*

Or perhaps I don't... Anyway, while we wait, we can concentrate
on something more pleasant than a mob of squabbling savages.

ULYSSES

Go ahead, go ahead!

HOMER

Now, that's hardly the frame of mind for listening—

ULYSSES

I said I'd hear you out, didn't I?

HOMER

> *(Taking a seat by the fireplace, and facing the table)*

Well, don't interrupt me—let me finish the poem before you
start criticising. Now, you must imagine my harp on my knee.
But at the moment, I shan't sing: I must keep my voice fresh for
this evening.

ULYSSES

(Genuinely angry)

You mean to sing at the banquet? For that bunch of cutthroats?

HOMER

I shall sing for Penelope. It may be the last song I shall sing, the last she will hear.

(ULYSSES is silenced. HOMER's voice loses its emotion and becomes practical again.)

I strike a few chords in a minor key; then I slide into a major chord—the Odysseus motif, which reappears throughout the poem.

ULYSSES

(Impatiently, his eyes watching the door)

Yes, yes...

HOMER

(Begins his narration. He is impressive and noble. His audience, who have been watching the door, gradually turn their eyes toward the poet. They sit or stand quite motionless, in the gathering dusk.)

As soon as early dawn appeared,
The rosy-fingered dawn, touching earth into life,
They all set out for the hunt—the hounds and the men.
And with them went the young Odysseus.
Up the green hill they climbed, steeply to wind-swept ridges
Furred with trees.
Then the baying of hounds, the trampling of men's feet
Came to the boar as he slept in still shadow,

And he sprang from his lair, his crest bristling,
His cunning eyes aflame; and he stood, waiting, motionless,
But Odysseus saw him, and moved in swiftly, his spear upraised.

CLIA
(Quickly)
It was a *knife* he held.

HOMER
It was a *spear*! Nobody could hunt a wild boar with a knife!
*(ULYSSES smiles and shakes his head. And then looks
at the door as he hears the sounds of horses, coming
nearer. HOMER resumes, and TELEMACHUS, EUMAEUS, and
CLIA watch him.)*
Then the boar twisted sideways, ripped deep with his tusk,
driving a gash above the hunter's knee.

CLIA
(In quiet exasperation)
Below his knee.

HOMER
(Gives her an angry look)
But Odysseus aimed well, and struck with all his force—
*(Now there are sounds from the courtyard, outside, of
men and horses.)*
And the shining point of the bright spear went gleaming through.
*(MELAS, dishevelled somewhat, appears silently in the
doorway. Behind him, the yard is bathed in a golden sunset.)*
And the boar fell—

MELAS

(Angrily, as he takes a step into the Hall, drawing his sword, looking around searchingly)

Where's Eryx? Where is he?

ULYSSES

How should we know? We're listening to Homer.

MELAS

The perfect audience—a pig-keeper, a boy, and a beggar—listening at sunset to an old wife's tale! Get the torches lit!

CLIA

It's too early—it's a waste—

MELAS

Light them!

(CLIA, at a small sign from ULYSSES, goes over to the fire, to ignite a long taper and start lighting the nearest torches on the fireplace wall. Meanwhile, MELAS goes on speaking. He has taken a step toward the dais, looks up toward the door to PENELOPE'S room. ULYSSES rises, as MELAS moves. At that moment, ATHENA appears from downstage right and stands very still, behind ULYSSES. MELAS points with his sword.)

Is he up there, with Penelope?

ATHENA

(As ULYSSES reaches for his knife)

Wait, Ulysses, wait!

TELEMACHUS
(Rushing forward, his knife out)
Keep away from there, or I'll—

MELAS
(Swings round to meet TELEMACHUS, *catches his upraised wrist, twists the knife out of his hand, shoves him back, and picks up the knife to slip into his belt)*
You'll what, sonny?
*(*TELEMACHUS, *still defiant but watching the sword, is moving along the wall to the left of the door, in order to reach the steps to* PENELOPE'S *room.* EUMAEUS *is moving too, quietly, keeping close to the right wall to try to reach* MELAS *from that side of the Hall. By the hearth,* HOMER *sits, watchful and ready, while* CLIA *seems frozen as she stands, taper in hand.* ATHENA *has one arm held out, as if restraining* ULYSSES, *who has taken a step forward.* MELAS, *unaware of all this as he turns his back on them to keep his eyes on* TELEMACHUS, *suddenly notices the Great Bow, which is now behind the boy as he moves toward the steps to the dais.)*
Who has touched that bow? It has been moved. Eryx—
(He slashes with his sword at it, as TELEMACHUS *dodges toward the steps, and the bow falls to the ground.)*
Yes, Eryx tried that bow, didn't he?
*(*ULYSSES *drops back onto the bench.* ATHENA'S *arm falls. All movement stops as* MELAS *whirls round to face them again.)*
Didn't he?

ULYSSES

(Unconcerned, bored)

Stop shouting. We can hear you.

(His calm voice acts as a signal to the others. CLIA lights the taper and goes on with her job. The rest remain where they are, silent.)

MELAS

So he did try that bow! And then?

ULYSSES

He didn't tell us much. Secretive kind of fellow. Oh, he did say you nearly got smashed to pulp, up on the mountain. A crag fell.

MELAS

And why didn't you bring help?

ULYSSES

Help? Did someone get hurt?

MELAS

(Grimly)

A man is dead, because no help—See here, I'm asking the questions.

ULYSSES

(Smiling)

Then you'd better start asking who gave that crag a push. It was meant for you, wasn't it? Kind of lucky you jumped aside.

MELAS

(Quite still, staring at ULYSSES*)*

Stay here, all of you... Clia, get their knives! Gather them in your apron! Bring them here!

*(*CLIA *hesitates, taper in hand.)*

Or else—!

(He threatens TELEMACHUS *with his sword, for a moment.* ULYSSES *pulls his cloak back, just enough to let him take his knife out. He places it on the table behind him.* CLIA *drops the taper, and moves quickly across the Hall to the table, to collect the knife.* EUMAEUS, *grumbling, comes forward to hand over his knife.)*

That's what I call reasonable. And remember, anyone found wandering outside is liable to get hurt.

(The sun has set. The yard is darkening. PHILETIUS *enters quietly, slipping around the side of the big door, his hand going to his knife in his belt.)*

Like this one, here!

*(*MELAS *whips round, as he speaks, to strike* PHILETIUS *on the right arm with his sword, and the knife falls to the ground.* MELAS *laughs as he puts his foot on it, and* PHILETIUS*, his right arm badly wounded, stumbles toward* TELEMACHUS*.)*

Don't forget *your* knives, Clia!

CLIA

(Turns back to the table to pick up two kitchen knives to add to her apron)

How can I cook for you, without a knife to cut?

MELAS

That's your problem.

(He grins as she comes toward him with her apron bundled
around the knives. He points to the knife at his feet.)

And this one, too.

(She picks it up, adds it to the apron.)

Drop that bundle down the well! Then come back here.

ULYSSES

(As CLIA hesitates)

Why argue with a sword? Do as he says, old woman.

(CLIA goes out.)

MELAS

(Almost genial, now)

That's what I like—co-operation.

(The three men who had come down the mountain
with MELAS appear at the door.)

Well—did you find Eryx? And the others?

FIRST MAN

Not a sign. Their horses are here, but they've vanished.

MELAS

(Grimly)

We'll find them...

(To ULYSSES)

You seem to have sense. Keep them quiet! When we return, I
want to see this Hall blazing with light, the food and wine set
out, and Penelope—there! At my right hand.

(His sword points to the head of the table. MELAS *and his friends leave abruptly.* ULYSSES *has risen to his feet, his hands clenched.* MELAS' *voice shouts a command to* CLIA.*)*

Get inside!

*(*CLIA *stumbles forward into the Hall as if she had been roughly pushed.)*

ATHENA

Even I am surprised by so much restraint, Ulysses. Congratulations!

*(*ULYSSES *unclenches his fists, walks slowly over to the hearth. He looks at no one. They all look at him, accusingly.* CLIA *is totally bewildered as she moves to the table, and stands there, helpless.* EUMAEUS *crosses quickly to the steps where* TELEMACHUS *is trying to help* PHILETIUS.*)*

TELEMACHUS

(Forgetting that ULYSSES *is playing the beggar for* HOMER's *benefit)*

You could have stopped him. Why didn't you—

(He remembers, and stops.)

HOMER

(Rising, avoiding ULYSSES*)*

Why?—Would a man be a beggar, if he had any courage?

(He sighs and looks around.)

Now what?—I have a small knife in my room, somewhere or other. But quite useless, I'm afraid.

(He sighs again, and moves very markedly away from ULYSSES, *toward the table.* ULYSSES *signs to* CLIA *to get the old boy out of the Hall.)*

CLIA

(To HOMER*)*

What you need right now is a drink.

(She pours him some wine.)

HOMER

No... No, thanks...

CLIA

Just one sip. You'll feel much better.

(She hands him the cup of wine.)

HOMER

Look after Philetius: he needs your attention more than I do.

(But he takes the cup and drinks eagerly.)

CLIA

I don't think he does, somehow. You're an *awful* responsibility,
Homer. What are the people of Greece going to say about us,
when they hear we got you killed?

*(She goes over to one of the chests, opens it, takes out
a piece of linen, and starts tearing it into strips.)*

HOMER

Well, if I can face death with a little of the courage I've always
praised—at least they can write on my tombstone: Here lies a
poet who practised what he preached.

*(He shudders, and then tries to laugh. He drains the
cup and sets it down on the table.* CLIA *watches him as
she prepares the bandages.)*

I think I'll go and search for that little knife of mine, such as it is.

CLIA

And why not rest?

HOMER
(Now almost reaching the door to the men's quarters)
Call me. Call me when I'm needed. Suddenly—I feel very tired.
(The door closes behind him.)

ULYSSES
(Rising quickly, throwing away his cloak, moving swiftly toward PHILETIUS*)*
How bad is it, eh?
(He examines the wound.)
Better come over here, where there's some light.
(Puts his arm around PHILETIUS' *shoulders and draws him toward the hearth, where the torches have been lit. The rest of the Hall is shadowed, now, and the yard outside is quite dark.* ULYSSES *gives a brief order to* EUMAEUS.*)*
You stay near the door. Keep your eyes and ears open. Clia, where's that bandage?
(To PHILETIUS, *with a grin)*
Did success go to your head—coming in here, without scouting around first? Mission accomplished, I take it.
*(*PHILETIUS *nods.)*

TELEMACHUS

(Hovering around anxiously)

Oh Jupiter!—If you could only give him back his tongue!

ULYSSES

(Kneeling beside PHILETIUS, *who is now sitting on the*
stool beside the hearth, examining the arm under the
torchlight, taking the bandage from CLIA)

He doesn't need a tongue. The knives did all the talking
necessary. He took two with him. He brought one back.

*(*PHILETIUS *nods.* ULYSSES *waves* CLIA *away.)*

I've learned how to do this, Clia. Go to Penelope. Stay with her.
Keep her quiet. And don't let her come down into this Hall.

CLIA

But—

ATHENA

(Moving away from downstage right, where she has been
standing quite motionless, walking obliquely across the
Hall toward the steps to the dais, passing close to CLIA,
who stands hesitating in the centre of the stage)

He's right, Clia. You know Penelope—she's getting restless.
She'll be down here any minute, to see what is going on.

CLIA

(To ULYSSES)

She'll ask questions.

ULYSSES

Then answer them.

CLIA

(Going toward the steps where ATHENA *waits for her)*
But what shall I tell her?

ULYSSES

Tell her I've been practising. She needn't worry about the contest. Everything is under control. I hope.

CLIA

Is that all I can tell her?
                    (She has now reached the dais.)

ULYSSES

The less she knows, the less she'll worry.

CLIA

(Hesitating at the door to the women's quarters)
I'd rather face Melas than this.
            (She goes out. ATHENA *almost follows her, looks back
            at* ULYSSES, *pauses, and then compromises by standing
            on the dais in front of* PENELOPE's *door.)*

ULYSSES

(To EUMAEUS, *who is still standing very close to one side
                of the big doorway)*
Anyone out there?

EUMAEUS

The courtyard's clear. They are searching the barns now.

ULYSSES

(*To* TELEMACHUS)

Get out the swords.

(*He finishes bandaging the arm.*)

What took you so long to get back here? You had me worried.

(PHILETIUS *makes quick signs with his left hand, pointing
eastward to the fireplace wall.*)

You came home by the shore?

(PHILETIUS *nods.*)

You scouted round the Bay?

(PHILETIUS *nods.*)

Did you see any signs of Eryx? How many men with him?

(PHILETIUS *nods, holds up four fingers.*)

Were they setting sail?

(PHILETIUS *shakes his head.*)

Still waiting?... For what? He must know something has
happened to his scout by this time...

(ULYSSES *rises quickly, paces worriedly. To* PHILETIUS *again*)

You made sure the man was dead?

(PHILETIUS *draws a finger across his throat.*)

ATHENA

(*Calling gently over to* ULYSSES, *as he paces to the table,
pauses there, turns*)

You dangled a carrot in front of Eryx's nose; why not try a
stick, now?

ULYSSES
(Staring thoughtfully at the ground)
An added incentive—that's what is needed.
(He snaps his fingers, looks up at PHILETIUS *again.)*
Your arm is useless, but how are your legs?
*(*ULYSSES *begins to smile, as he meets* PHILETIUS *in the centre of the Hall.* TELEMACHUS *has already opened the chest concealing the weapons, and sorted them out on the floor.)*
Slip outside. Let Melas and his men get a glimpse of you. Then run! Run like hell—to the Bay. Make sure they follow, like a pack of hounds in full cry. Just let Eryx hear them, coming toward the boat, and he'll set sail in a hurry.
(As ULYSSES *speaks, he gives* PHILETIUS *a farewell clap on his back, and crosses to the hearth to light two tapers.* PHILETIUS *only stops to lift a knife from* TELEMACHUS' *hand, and slips round the side of the door into the darkness of the yard.)*

TELEMACHUS
(Picking up a sword, following PHILETIUS*)*
I'll go with him. I want to be there when that boat—

ULYSSES
(Sharply, and yet not loudly, so that his voice will not carry outside)
Stay here! You can start lighting the torches. You, too, Eumaeus!
(He goes toward the door, hands them each a taper.)
We'll give Melas that one wish, at least.

TELEMACHUS

But—

ULYSSES

(Already pushing stools nearer the walls, shoving
benches closer to the table but leaving the head chair
angled out to face the Hall)

I said I needed you here!

(EUMAEUS is already lighting the torches on one wall.
TELEMACHUS begins on another wall.)

TELEMACHUS

I only wanted to see—

ULYSSES

(Still clearing the floor space)

You'll see plenty, out in that courtyard with Eumaeus. That's
where I want you to wait. Keep in the shadows. Stay hidden.
When Melas and his men return—

TELEMACHUS

We'll trap them!

ULYSSES

(Very sharply, yet not loudly)

No! Let them pass into the Hall.

TELEMACHUS

But we could ambush them, out there.

ULYSSES

And scatter them? In this darkness, we'd never round them up.
(He has moved over to the fallen bow, picks it up,
looks at it sadly.)

No, I want them *here*, all of them.
(He throws the bow, like a spear, angrily, at the quiver
with its four meagre arrows lying beside the opened chest.)

Your job is to cut off any retreat from the Hall. Got that?
(There is a shout, outside, as PHILETIUS has let himself
be seen, and a sudden clatter of running feet, going
farther and farther away.)

Quick! Get in position—now!
(EUMAEUS picks up a sword and moves to the door,
waits for TELEMACHUS.)

Out!
(Suddenly, in a roar of command)

Jump to it!
(TELEMACHUS moves to the door, grips his sword, and
enters the yard.)

EUMAEUS

(As ULYSSES watches his son leave)
I'll keep him safe, Ulysses.
(ULYSSES grasps the old man's shoulder, and then
EUMAEUS hurries after the boy.)

ULYSSES

(Watches them go, looks at the quiet darkness of the
courtyard for a moment. Then he turns away, grim-
faced. He speaks angrily.)

This isn't the time for emotion—or fear—or worry.

(He moves toward the open chest, and the scattered weapons.)

ATHENA

(With her hand on the door that leads to the women's quarters)

Not even a time for reflection. All you need now, Ulysses, is a quick eye, a strong arm, and a brave heart.

(She watches him as he picks up a sword and tests its weight. He chooses another, carefully.)

You have them all. And I can't take any credit for them. I'm not even supposed to admire them. Yet, strange—strange that I can almost love men when they face this moment in their lives. Ulysses—you are bad for me. Let me go to Penelope, and become the cold, calm goddess again…

(She opens the door and goes through, closing it quietly.)

ULYSSES

(Fastening the sword to his belt, and then selecting a couple of throwing knives)

I could be wrong, all wrong. Perhaps Philetius stumbled, and then Melas would be on him like a wolf. Or Eryx—he could have changed his plans. Scoundrels are unpredictable: they fall out, yes; but they can join forces again when you least expect it…

(He secures the knives at his waist.)

Well—too late, now, to worry about all that. There never was a battle yet, when I didn't feel nervous to begin with…

(From the distance, come excited shouts. At this, he moves quickly to the wall on the right side of the door, where the shields are hanging.)

I'd be happier if I could find my old shield. What have they done with it?

(He searches the wall with his eyes.)

All this damned house-cleaning each spring. Clia never leaves a thing in place.

(He has taken down a round shield, leather-covered.)

I remember this one. A bit on the small side, after what I've been using. No, no, no. The weight's all wrong.

(He rejects it.)

Besides, I'll need both hands free if I use the knives.

(He moves back to the hearth, nervous and restless. On impulse, he picks up a piece of charred wood, and adds a second stroke to the wall.)

Lucas, the sacrificial goat... That's certain, anyway... What about Eryx, himself, and his four men in that boat? Why not?

(He laughs and scores five more times.)

Well, I'll soon know—definitely. If Eryx walks in here with Melas, then—

(He throws away his marker, smiles grimly.)

I'll really have a fight on my hands.

(He turns abruptly to face the door as he hears the brief warning of an owl hooting. There is the sound of footsteps in the yard. Suddenly, they are hushed. Silence.)

MELAS

(Entering suddenly, quietly, looking around the Hall, his sword drawn. He calls back, over his shoulder, to the men following him.)

There's only the beggar here. I'll deal with him. You search for the boy and the pig-keeper.

(He comes further into the Hall.)

You seem to be amused. Why? Because Eryx and his men have sailed away… Let me amuse you more, my friend.

(He raises his sword. He is quiet, confident, contemptuous.)

ULYSSES

(His smile broadening)

My arithmetic wasn't so bad, after all.

(He points to his score marks.)

A poor joke, I admit; but there are worse ways to enter a fight than with a smile on your lips.

MELAS

So you're going to fight, are you? I'll fight no beggar. But I'll string your nose and ears as a decoration around your neck.

(ULYSSES, still smiling, draws himself to his full height, and brings his sword up on guard.)

You'd like some lessons in how to use a sword? What's your usual weapon? A stick, or an axe?

(ULYSSES parries a thrust easily; another, and another.
MELAS' bluster is now over. He is watchful, dangerous.)

Who are you, anyway?

ULYSSES

You'll learn!

(He springs forward with a sudden shout. MELAS fights back, but is forced to give way. He gives a warning yell as he tries to reach the door, but ULYSSES fights round him and forces him back toward the long dining table.)

Take your favourite chair, Melas!

(He kills MELAS *at the foot of* ULYSSES' *chair, and then turns to face the three men who have come running in answer to* MELAS' *call. For a moment the men hesitate, as they see* MELAS *dead.)*

Come in, gentlemen! Welcome to *my* house!

ONE OF THE MEN
(Turning to run into the yard)

Ulysses!

(But as he turns, ULYSSES *pulls a knife from his belt and throws it after the fleeing man as he reaches the courtyard. His cry is heard from the darkness outside.)*

ULYSSES
(Sword ready, speaking softly)

Yes, it's Ulysses.

(He leaps forward to attack the two men. As the curtain closes, they are fighting back vigorously, dangerously.)

The curtain remains closed only for a brief space. From the hidden Hall, we can hear some shouts, then a hideous scream. Then silence...

SCENE 3

The Great Hall is empty. Its large entrance doors are closed.
The brightly lit torches flicker over the upset benches, the dark
stains on the floor. Silence. The door to the women's quarters
is thrown open, and PENELOPE *appears.* CLIA *follows, protesting,*
trying to pull PENELOPE *back toward her room.*

CLIA
(Angry)

Ulysses said you were to stay back in your own room!
Penelope—
> *(But* PENELOPE, *halting on the shallow step, looks round*
> *the Hall in fear.* CLIA *is silenced, as she looks, too.)*

PENELOPE

Something went wrong... I knew it. I knew it. Oh, Clia—
> *(She comes slowly down the steps into the Hall.)*

CLIA

(Runs down the steps, looks at the chair where MELAS *had been killed. A dark stain has gathered there. She points.)*
Blood—there!

PENELOPE

(Her voice is too quiet.)
Ulysses—they rushed Ulysses and killed him!

CLIA

(Sees two more dark patches)
And there, and there! Two more were killed—Telemachus? Eumaeus?
(She rushes to the entrance door, but cannot open it.)
They've barred the door. They've shut us inside.
(She stands panic-stricken.)

PENELOPE

(Tensely)
I knew it. As soon as I heard the screams, I knew something had gone wrong. And then, that terrible silence.
(Turns on CLIA*)*
Why did you keep me locked in my room? Why, why?

CLIA

(Sharply)
What use would you have been, down here?

PENELOPE

I could have died with Ulysses, with my son—
(She covers her face, stands hopeless.)

CLIA

Oh, Penelope, Penelope—what shall we do now?

HOMER
*(Struggling out of sleep, appears in the doorway of the
men's quarters. He carries a small knife. He lowers it,
self-consciously.)*

I must have fallen asleep—can you believe it, I fell asleep? Then
suddenly, a hideous scream, the scream of a death agony. Or
was it all part of some hidden dream?

PENELOPE
(Lifelessly)

It was no dream.

HOMER
*(He has slipped the small knife into his belt. He comes
forward, and begins to notice the room. He stares at
the dark stains on the floor. He awakens fully.)*

Who was killed here? Whose bodies have been dragged out
to the yard? There has been a fight—who—whom? Clia, why
didn't you waken me, why did you let me sleep?

CLIA

(Still at the entrance door, listening)

I thought I heard wheels—a cart being driven away. A cart? Are they taking the bodies away? To throw over the cliff?

(She begins to weep.)

PENELOPE

(In horror)

Clia!

CLIA

That's what they did with the others they killed, three years ago. That's what they—

PENELOPE

(Tensely)

Stop that!

(She faces HOMER.)

It's all over. We are prisoners. You, Clia, and I.

HOMER

Where is the boy? Old Eumaeus? The beggar? Are they dead?

PENELOPE

(Dully)

Yes... Ulysses is dead.

HOMER

Ulysses? Odysseus is dead? *Odysseus?*

PENELOPE
(Beginning to weep)

Ulysses was the beggar, Homer. He had a plan—it didn't work. And *I* am to blame for all this. I started it all, but I never meant it to end this way.

CLIA
(Her voice is harsh, bitter.)

You never meant it to end this way? When you throw a stone down a mountainside, does it fall on a ledge and stay there? Or does it go on falling, carrying other stones with it, starting a rockslide?

HOMER
(To CLIA, as he goes toward PENELOPE, and puts his arm round her)

Quiet, woman, quiet!
(He sees the big bow lying on the floor, then the quiver and fallen arrows.)

CLIA
(Still angry)

One spoken word, and the stone is thrown. One small gesture, and the rockslide is moving. And you think it can be stopped by an apology?
(Chants bitterly)
I was wrong, I didn't know, I never meant it—Bah!

HOMER

(Goes over to the bow, picks up an arrow)

Quiet! You help no one. We must think...

PENELOPE

(Follows him)

Think? I've done too much thinking. I invented a contest. A contest? Ulysses didn't even have time to use that bow. He was cut down—

(She can't go on.)

HOMER

But there are only four arrows... A quiver holds more than that. Perhaps he did account for some of those ruffians before the rest rushed at him. Perhaps—

(He sighs, heavily, sadly.)

We'll never know what really happened.

PENELOPE

(Picks up a dagger from the chest where ULYSSES *had hidden the weapons)*

This is all that is left.

HOMER

I'll take that, Penelope.

PENELOPE

(Suddenly asserting herself)

No. I have a use for it. You go back to your room, Homer. Stay there, please.

HOMER

And leave you to face these men, alone?

PENELOPE

(Comes back to centre stage)

Please go, Clia! Get the spear in my room—Ulysses' spear. Get it!

CLIA

(Listening, pressed against the door)

I hear a rumble of wheels. They've come back.

PENELOPE

Get that spear!

(As CLIA *leaves the door and runs up the steps toward* PENELOPE'S *room,* HOMER *comes over quietly to stand beside* PENELOPE *in the centre of the Hall.)*

Oh, Homer! You could save yourself. They have no quarrel with you.

HOMER

I suppose they'd leave me alive if I were to turn my *Odyssey* into a poem praising them. But—I'd rather it stayed unfinished.

(Very sadly)

It was to have been a happy story—one that ended pleasantly, encouragingly

PENELOPE

Instead—I have turned it into a tragedy.

HOMER
(Sombrely)

Then you are a true Greek, Penelope... Why do our stories always have to end in tragedy?
(He sighs.)

The fault, dear lady, lies not in our stars, but in ourselves—
(The door's heavy bar is being raised from outside. HOMER takes out his knife and places his other hand on PENELOPE's shoulder as they turn defiantly to face the opening door. PENELOPE's hand, holding the dagger, is at her back, half hidden by her skirt. ULYSSES enters, and halts. Behind him are TELEMACHUS, EUMAEUS, and PHILETIUS, excited and triumphant.)

ULYSSES
(To PENELOPE)

And what the hell are you doing down here?

PENELOPE
(Almost faints against HOMER, who holds her for a moment. She pushes him away, and runs to ULYSSES.)

I thought they had killed you. I thought you were dead.

ULYSSES
(Catching her into his arms)

Kill this old fox? Not likely. I knew a trick or two they hadn't even thought of.
(He suddenly notices CLIA, with the spear, at the top of the steps.)

Have you women gone crazy, or something? What chance do you think you would have had?

(Takes the dagger out of PENELOPE'*s hand)*

And who was this meant for?

(Throws the dagger aside and laughs and embraces
PENELOPE *again)*

HOMER
(Coming forward)

Odysseus!

TELEMACHUS

Oh, Mother, he was wonderful! You should have seen him, Clia!—What are you staring at?

CLIA

Ghosts.

(She drops the spear and comes slowly down the steps.)

HOMER

(He and ULYSSES *grasp hands.* ULYSSES *keeps one arm
around* PENELOPE, *never lets her go.)*

This ghost feels very solid to me. Odysseus—welcome! Home is the hunter, home from the hill, and the sailor home from sea!

ULYSSES

(Looking around, still holding PENELOPE)

And home to stay, this time. I'd never risk another night like this one.

(He looks at PENELOPE. CLIA *has started to straighten things.)*

Leave that to morning, Clia. Let's all move toward bed. Is no one tired, around here, except me?

CLIA

But is it safe to go to bed? Are they—are they all dead?

ULYSSES
(Cheerfully)

Not one left. We can sleep in peace. Now—let's say good night—

HOMER
(Insistent)

One man against eleven! But how—?

ULYSSES
(Gestures to TELEMACHUS)

I had some useful help.

TELEMACHUS
(Proudly)

Oh... I didn't do much. Eumaeus and I—we just sort of guarded the door, cut off all retreat.

ULYSSES

You stood ready. You didn't give ground. That's something, boy.

HOMER
(Determined)

But *how* did you—?

ULYSSES
(Brusquely)
It was a free-for-all, crazy, mixed up. Began suddenly, and then—well, it was over. That's all.

HOMER
So that's all, is it? I don't believe a word you say. It must have been an epic fight. Heroic! You took your own house as you captured Troy! Come—tell me it all. I want to hear the details while they are still fresh in your mind.

ULYSSES
(Drawing PENELOPE *toward the steps)*
Tomorrow will be time enough for that. Or the day after tomorrow.
(He smiles broadly.)
Get some sleep, all of you. And don't waken me for a week!

HOMER
But I've never been more wide awake in my life...
(Suddenly noticing ULYSSES' *impatience)*
Sorry... Of course—tomorrow will do... I suppose.
(He looks dashed. Then he sees TELEMACHUS *picking up
the bow to replace on the wall, and goes to help him.)*
This bow saw some hard service tonight, didn't it?

TELEMACHUS
Well—

HOMER
(Taking TELEMACHUS' arm)

Come, let's walk a little in the cool, free air. It will clear our heads, and you can give me all the details. Tell me how and why and where. If I didn't see the climax to this story, I can at least hear about it. And, listening, I'll see it as clearly as if I had been there.

ULYSSES
(Halting at the steps, worried)

Telemachus—

TELEMACHUS

Don't worry.

ULYSSES
(Warningly)

No embroidery!

(Laughs)

Leave that to your mother.

TELEMACHUS
(Grinning)

I'll tell Homer exactly what he wants to know.

HOMER

Splendid. Now, the Great Bow is what interests me most. Let's begin with that incident, and I'll make it the grand climax of the *Odyssey*.

(He walks out with TELEMACHUS, *talking, talking.*)

EUMAEUS
(Catching PHILETIUS' *arm)*

I wouldn't miss this for anything. Let's see if Telemachus can spin as good a yarn as his father. And I've got some details of my own to add.

(They look at ULYSSES *with a broad grin and start moving into the courtyard.* CLIA *looks at* ULYSSES *and* PENELOPE, *who have forgotten her. She pulls a shawl over her shoulders.)*

CLIA

And what about mine? I was the first to recognise Ulysses, wasn't I? Besides, this is the first night in three years I can walk out in the fresh, free air.

(She hurries after the others. Their laughing voices fade into the gentle night. ATHENA *has entered as they leave, and—as she speaks—comes downstage.)*

ATHENA

There's no place for Reason, out there. They will catch cold, but what does that matter when the air *is* free, and one can laugh again?

(As PENELOPE *breaks away from a long embrace,* ATHENA *halts downstage, right, and turns to watch them.* PENELOPE *looks toward the courtyard.)*

PENELOPE

Poor Homer—they'll confuse him, completely.

ULYSSES
(Laughing)

Not Homer. He'll confuse them until they believe everything he says.

PENELOPE

What *is* the true story of tonight, Ulysses?

ULYSSES
(Tenderly)

You and I.

PENELOPE

You didn't use the Great Bow, did you?

ULYSSES
(After a pause)

No. I didn't. But does that matter?

PENELOPE
(Laughing)

Nothing matters except—you are home. And you love me.
(She throws her arms round her husband.)
And you didn't lie to me. Oh, Ulysses, Ulysses!
(They kiss, a long long kiss. ATHENA has lost interest. She is walking across the stage, and a transparent curtain moves with her. She holds its edge with an upraised arm, as if she were drawing it closed. As she walks, she looks out over the audience, smiling, speaking.)

ATHENA

See? No place for Reason here, either. Nothing for me to do, now. Except, perhaps, to draw a veil... So good night, my friends. Good night, Ulysses. Good night, my sweet Penelope. Your story will last *three* thousand years and more. Was that worth waiting for, Penelope? Good night, good night...

(Her voice fades as she leaves, downstage left.)

The Great Hall is veiled. The lights dim. The veil becomes opaque and forms the

CURTAIN

ABOUT THE AUTHOR

Helen MacInnes, whom the *Sunday Express* called 'the Queen of spy writers', was the author of many distinguished suspense novels.

Born in Scotland, she studied at the University of Glasgow and University College, London, then went to Oxford after her marriage to Gilbert Highet, the eminent critic and educator. In 1937 the Highets went to New York, and except during her husband's war service, Helen MacInnes lived there ever since.

Since her first novel *Above Suspicion* was published in 1941 to immediate success, all her novels have been bestsellers; *The Salzburg Connection* was also a major film.

Helen MacInnes died in September 1985.

PRAISE FOR HELEN MacINNES

"The queen of spy writers." *Sunday Express*

"Definitely in the top class." *Daily Mail*

"The hallmarks of a MacInnes novel of suspense are as individual and as clearly stamped as a Hitchcock thriller." *The New York Times*

"A sophisticated thriller. The story builds up to an exciting climax." *Times Literary Supplement*

"Absorbing, vivid, often genuinely terrifying." *Observer*

"She can hang her cloak and dagger right up there with Eric Ambler and Graham Greene." *Newsweek*

"An atmosphere that is ready to explode with tension... a wonderfully readable book." *The New Yorker*

PRAISE FOR DONALD HAMILTON

"Hamilton has brought to the spy novel the authentic hard realism of Dashiell Hammett…probably as close to the sordid truth of espionage, as any now being told."
Anthony Boucher, *New York Times*

"This series by Donald Hamilton is the top-ranking American secret agent fare, with its intelligent protagonist and an author who consistently writes in high style. Good writing, slick plotting and stimulating characters, all tartly flavored with wit." *Book Week*

"The appearance of a new Matt Helm story is always good news." *Chicago Tribune*

"Fast, tightly written, brutal, and very good…"
Milwaukee Journal

"With Matt Helm, Donald Hamilton helped start the spy adventure genre. I welcome the reissue of these books so that readers can experience this mythic hero."
David Morrell, *New York Times* bestselling author of *Murder as Fine Art*

THE HARRY HOUDINI MYSTERIES

BY DANIEL STASHOWER

The Dime Museum Murders
The Floating Lady Murder
The Houdini Specter

In turn-of-the-century New York, the Great Houdini's confidence in his own abilities is matched only by the indifference of the paying public. Now the young performer has the opportunity to make a name for himself by attempting the most amazing feats of his fledgling career—solving what seem to be impenetrable crimes. With the reluctant help of his brother Dash, Houdini must unravel murders, debunk frauds and escape from danger that is no illusion...